WORKHOUSE

St Marylebone Workhouse and Institution (1730-1965)
by Alan R Neate
First published by St Marylebone Society 1967.
Revised edition 2003 published by the St Marylebone Society, City of Westminster Archives Centre and the University of Westminster.

The revisions to the 1967 text by Alan R Neate relate solely to changes in the names of streets, responsible public authorities and the use of buildings. This has been done to make the text more easily understandable to present-day readers. Selected illustrations that appeared in the original edition have been supplemented by others from the City of Westminster Archives Centre.

Copyright St Marylebone Society, City of Westminster Archives Centre and the University of Westminster, 2003.

ISBN 1-900893-13-4

The illustrations appearing on pp 58 and 59 are reproduced by kind permission of London Metropolitan Archives.

Copies of this and other publications are obtainable from Westminster Archives Centre, 10 St Ann's Street, London SW1P 2DE (Tel: 020 7641 5180)

The cover illustration is of the Infirmary to the Workhouse, built in 1792 to the north west of the main building. Watercolour, 1803.

Produced by Historical Publications Ltd, 32 Ellington Street, London N7 8PL (Tel: 020 7607 1628)
Printed by Witley Press, Hunstanton, Norfolk

ST MARYLEBONE WORKHOUSE
and Institution, 1730-1965

Alan R Neate BSc (Econ) DPA ACCS
Record Keeper to the Greater London Council

St Marylebone Society
City of Westminster Archives
University of Westminster

Contents

AUTHOR'S FOREWORD	5
ST MARYLEBONE WORKHOUSE AND INSTITUTION 1730-1965, BY ALAN R NEATE	6
ENDNOTES	56
APPENDIX A: DIET TABLES AT ST MARYLEBONE WORKHOUSE IN 1846	between pp 56 & 57
APPENDIX B: MASTERS OF ST MARYLEBONE WORKHOUSE AND WARDENS OF LUXBOROUGH LODGE SINCE 1775	57
AFTERWORD BY BRENDA WEEDEN, UNIVERSITY OF WESTMINSTER ARCHIVIST	58
INDEX	62

Author's Foreword

In 1965 there disappeared from the St Marylebone scene a large London County Council welfare home occupying a four acre site opposite the famous waxworks of Madame Tussaud and known as Luxborough Lodge. It had received this designation, by way of re-christening, in 1949, when the Council, desirous of registering the break with the past represented by the 'Welfare State' and the changed social attitudes of which it was the expression, had decided to give new names to the older institutions inherited from the former poor-law authorities nineteen years previously. For this was the St Marylebone Workhouse and Institution and the buildings demolished in 1965 were the result of the large-scale reconstruction carried out by the St Marylebone Board of Guardians in stages between 1875 and 1901. There had, however, been a workhouse on the site continuously since 1775, and this in turn was the successor to institutions of a similar character, if smaller in size, in adjacent situations dating back some forty years earlier.

For some considerable part of its long and varied history the St Marylebone Workhouse was the largest of its kind in the country in terms of the population it housed. Erected before the full impact of the Industrial Revolution had made itself felt and when Marylebone was only just emerging as a fashionable suburb of London, ousting the predominantly rural community of earlier days, it saw the replacement of the older Poor Law by the harsher regime of the early nineteenth century, the gradual development of a more enlightened and humanitarian approach to the problems of poverty as the century moved to its close, the final break-up of the Poor Law and the emergence of the Welfare State. Each change which took place in the social scene was reflected in its own history, its use changed with the changing character and needs of the community at large and, when at last it disappeared, it did so because it had outlived the purpose for which it was created.

Its history is, therefore, in a real sense, a history of the Poor Law at its best and at its worst, and the present work is an attempt to place that history on record, now that the institution is no more.

The Author and the St Marylebone Society desire to acknowledge their gratitude to the City of Westminster and the University of Westminster for making a substantial grant towards the cost of publication.

Note concerning sources

The principal sources of information for the earliest period are the minutes of St Marylebone Vestry and its Committees, now in the custody of Westminster City Council at the City of Westminster Archives Centre, and the minutes of the Directors and Guardians of the Poor of St Marylebone and their 'Rota' Committee, now in the custody of London Metropolitan Archives. The latter office also houses the minutes and other records of the post-1867 St Marylebone Board of Guardians and of the London County Council and their various committees and sub-committees. The Ashbridge Collection at City of Westminster Archives Centre contains several drawings and prints of the workhouse. The author is particularly indebted to Dr FHW Sheppard's admirable *Local Government in St Marylebone, 1688-1835*. Many other works have also been consulted, some of which are mentioned in the text.

The Beginnings of the Workhouse, 1730-1752

When the question of providing a workhouse in St Marylebone first began to be mooted in the third and fourth decades of the eighteenth century, the parish was still predominantly rural in character, although the built-up area of the Metropolis had already crossed its southern boundary, which ran along Oxford Street, and was beginning to advance northwards. Maitland, writing only slightly later in his *History of London* in 1739, estimated the number of houses in Marylebone at 577, a figure which was to increase to 7,764 by the time of the 1801 Census, and Rocque's map of 1741-45 shows the village clustered about the thoroughfare which is known to this day as Marylebone High Street and with fields around it but with the encroaching development from the south already reaching a point just north of Cavendish Square.

In these circumstances, the administration of the poor law within its old Elizabethan framework had presented few problems and the first impetus towards providing indoor relief, when it came, arose not from any urgently pressing local need but rather from the growing conviction among enlightened circles that such a provision made for economy and efficiency in practice and, in particular, ensured some return for the outlay of the poor rate by way of the fruits of pauper labour. Workhouses were no novelty. The first in London, if one excludes such establishments as Bridewell and various houses of correction for vagrants, was probably that established in the neighbouring parish of St Giles-in-the-Fields in 1641. The success of the Bristol Workhouse after 1697 and those of Worcester, Plymouth, Norwich and other large towns, which followed in its wake, led in 1723 to the passing of the Poor Relief Act (Knatchbull's Act), which empowered parishes, if they wished, to hire or purchase premises for use as poorhouses and to refuse outdoor relief to paupers refusing to enter them. This Act may be taken as the starting point of indoor relief in St Marylebone.

Under its provisions and within seven years of its passage, the Vestry hired its first poorhouse, although it seems probable that this house was in fact only used to accommodate infants and their nurses without resident supervision. Later a large but dilapidated former alehouse in Marylebone Passage, known as the 'Golden Lion', was rented to house paupers of all categories. It was here that from 1736 on the typically eighteenth century expedient of 'farming the poor' was carried out. A contractor was paid two shillings[1] per week to take control of all the inmates and to pay the rent and all profit from their labour was retained by him. This arrangement and a number of variations of it over the succeeding years, however, proved far from successful. The general reluctance to enter the workhouse, even at the risk of forfeiting the right to outdoor relief by refusing to do so, and the unskilled nature of the labour of those who did enter it rendered it impossible for the contractor to make a profit or even to meet the commitments of rent and other expenses without substantial regular subsidies from the Vestry. The number of inmates was not at any time very large.

The First Permanent Workhouse, 1752 to 1775

The inadequacy of rented accommodation and the need to erect a permanent workhouse was quickly recognised. As early as 1731 the Earl of Oxford, in granting land to the parish for a new burial ground (now disused and turned into public gardens on the south side of Paddington Street) had made it a condition that six almshouses and a workhouse should be erected within seven years on part of the site. For financial reasons, however, the actual erection of a permanent workhouse did not commence until 1750, and it was not opened until two years later. This building stood in the north-east corner of the burial ground and consisted of a main block running parallel to Paddington Street with a wing at each end stretching forward to that thoroughfare at points roughly opposite the end of Northumberland Street (as the present Luxborough Street was called until the end of 1938). It was surrounded by high railings and was intended to house about forty paupers, a fact which makes it clear that the proposal was based upon the essentially small requirements of the still largely rural community.

A Workhouse Committee was now established with full powers to deal with all matters relating to the house and to poor relief generally, subject to the over-riding powers of the Vestry as its parent body. A Workhouse Master was appointed, but the traditions derived from the earlier farming of the poor died hard, and Francis Parent, the first Master, a former schoolmaster, was paid one shilling and sixpence[2] for each inmate each week, out of which he was to provide their

Advertisement for a Workhouse Master, 1768

food and the fruits of their labour were to be retained by him. In return, he undertook to teach the children reading, writing and arithmetic and to see that both children and adults were put to work in spinning or in winding silk. Within a period of months he requested unsuccessfully a rise of two pence[3] per head. His selection for the position was a singularly unfortunate one, for before a year had passed, complaints were being made of his drunkenness, frequent absences from the house, lack of discipline and misappropriation of supplies, as well as of his inability to control his own sons, one of whom was actually discovered in bed with a female inmate named Mary Salisbury. After Parent's dismissal, which immediately followed, his successors were paid a fixed salary of twenty pounds a year as simple employees. This removed some of the abuses but great difficulty continued to be experienced in finding persons really suited for the post.

Twenty-nine paupers entered the new workhouse on its

opening, of whom the overwhelming majority were children and nursing mothers. The inmates were subjected to a stringent regime which entailed work from 6 am to 8 pm with an hour's break for meals and, in the case of the children, two hours for schooling, and the Master was empowered to order punishments by way of curtailing rations or whipping in case of misconduct. The normal diet consisted of bread and cheese or broth for breakfast, boiled meat and suet pudding for dinner, hot and cold on alternate days, and bread and cheese for supper.

The workhouse proved from the start to be unsatisfactory. It became at an early date infested with rats from the sewers in the adjoining burial ground and it proved quite inadequate in size as the population mounted. The urbanisation of St Marylebone was now proceeding rapidly. In 1757 the New Road from Paddington to Islington, part of which is now known as Marylebone Road, came into being, and the development of the estates of the handful of wealthy and aristocratic landowners whose domains extended from Oxford Street to this new turnpike road followed quickly thereafter, gaining impetus after the restoration of peace when the Seven Years War ended in 1763. By the end of the century the village had been completely engulfed by one of the richest and most select residential areas of London and the population of the parish in the 1801 Census was 63,982.

Side by side with this development, there had been consequential changes in the administration of the parish. The old open vestry, at whose meetings the parishioners at large had been able to play their part in local affairs, disappeared in 1768 and with it the Committee of twenty whom they appointed to act, with the Churchwardens and the Overseers of the Poor, in day-to-day matters. The St Marylebone Select Vestry Act of 1768, passed by Parliament in pursuance of a petition organised by the aristocratic landowners of the parish, substituted a Select Vestry on the model already adopted in a number of other parishes, including the neighbouring one of St George's, Hanover Square. Ninety-nine men named in the Act, plus the Minister and the two Churchwardens, were to be Vestrymen, together with twenty other fit and substantial parishioners to be elected by them at their first meeting. Vacancies were to be filled by co-option as they occurred and the parishioners at large were thus excluded from participation. The effect was to broaden the basis of the body actually directing affairs to include not only the trades people who dominated the Committee of the Open Vestry, but also, in overwhelming majority, the nominees of the landowners who owned and leased the greater part of the property in the parish and demanded control over the policy of the Vestry. The Select Vestry proved very efficient in coping with the problems which urbanisation brought with it, and its one big defect, the lack of democratic control, did not become an issue until the uprise of radicalism and the Age of Reform sixty years later.

One of the first problems calling for attention was the handling of pauperism in the parish with its now swollen population. By 1772, when the number of inmates in the workhouse built for forty had reached two hundred and twenty, they were sleeping three and four to a bed. The addition of two extra storeys in that year and the hiring of a former public house called the 'Neptune' in the New Road to house the sick were inadequate measures to meet the situation and a new workhouse, conceived on a much larger scale, became an obvious necessity.

The New Workhouse in Northumberland Street

Thus it was that on 1 February 1774 the Vestry resolved unanimously "That it is the Opinion of this Vestry that the Building a large and Commodious Workhouse in this Parish would be a certain means of providing for and employing the Poor in a much more effectual and beneficial manner and also that much Money would be saved to the Parish by so doing. That in Order to carry this plan the better into Execution an application be forthwith made by this Vestry to His Grace the Duke of Portland acquainting his Grace with this Resolution and that his Grace would be pleased to take this matter into Consideration and signifye his Grace's pleasure to Grant by Lease or otherwise such Ground as may be commodious for the above purpose which must be of the greatest benefit and utility to this Parish." It was further resolved unanimously "That the Honourable and Reverend Mr Archdeacon Harley be requested to communicate the foregoing Resolution to his Grace the Duke of Portland."

It was not unnatural that in seeking a site the Vestry should turn to the Duke of Portland, for he was not only the principal landowner but also the lord of the manor. As a result of the Vestry's resolution, which Mr Archdeacon Harley obediently conveyed to him, a site was in due course provided, bounded by Northumberland Street and the New Road on the east and north and with the burial ground extension on the north side of Paddington Street as its southern boundary. This was to be the site of the workhouse for the next one hundred and ninety years. It was made up partly of land belonging to the Duke himself and partly of land belonging to Mr Henry Portman and was leased to the Vestry by them jointly on long leases. The leases were subsequently surrendered on two occasions, in 1791 and 1870, when new building operations were in contemplation, in favour of new leases on revised terms of ninety-nine years on the first occasion and eighty years in 1870. The freehold was ultimately purchased for £35,850[4] by agreement dated 14 May 1897, when the entire reconstruction of the workhouse was in process of being carried out and it was clearly inexpedient to build large and costly buildings on a site which might finally revert to the ground landlords.

To acquire the land and build and maintain a new workhouse, new statutory powers were deemed necessary and these were obtained by a special Act of Parliament in 1775 which prescribed in detail the arrangements for the relief of the poor in the parish. Its provisions, together with those of the other local Acts dealing with various aspects of the Vestry's work, were consolidated in the St Marylebone Vestry Act of 1795, which continued to provide the basis for the administration of poor relief until 1867. The Act of 1775 required the Vestry each year to appoint thirty parishioners as Directors and

The north front of the workhouse, c1780, with the south and west fronts, and chapel; water colour ascribed to John White, architect to the Duke of Portland, who designed the building in 1775.

Guardians of the Poor, an office which the Churchwardens were also to hold *ex officio*. The Directors and Guardians were to meet each quarter and on such other occasions as might be necessary and they were also to arrange themselves in six Committees of five which, in monthly rotation, would be successively responsible for the routine management of affairs, meeting once a week at the workhouse. The minutes of the proceedings of the Directors and Guardians and those of the Rota Committees throughout the period of their existence have survived in the custody of London Metropolitan Archives.

The new workhouse was commenced in 1775 and in the spring of the following year the inmates of the old building, numbering just under three hundred, were transferred to it. With an eye to future needs, it was designed for no less than a thousand inmates and took the form of a block fronting on Northumberland Street with two parallel blocks, extending westwards from points set in a little from its ends. In 1786, a chapel was added across the open space separating the ends of the two parallel blocks, so that the final effect was that of an enclosed rectangular quadrangle with a projecting block at each of the four corners. The whole was of two-storey stone construction and the total cost amounted to £18,770[5]. Its architect was John White, architect to the Duke of Portland.

The older workhouse was not immediately discarded but was taken into use as an infirmary to replace the rented house in the New Road, which was now purchased outright and demolished. Despite the alterations which were carried out and the efficient standards of treatment which resulted in a death-rate of less than half that prevailing in the best hospitals of the time, the building proved too small as the years progressed and its proximity to the burial ground led to periodical fever epidemics, the worst of which in 1791 killed both the matron and the apothecary. Dr William Rowley, who acted as physician to the Infirmary at this time, insisted that a new building on a different site was called for and the Vestry agreed to the allocation of part of the workhouse land leased from the Portland and Portman estates for this purpose. In this way, before the end of 1792, a brand new building with capacity for three hundred beds came into being to the north west of the workhouse; built, like the workhouse itself, in the form of an enclosed quadrangle. Dr Rowley, who was a firm believer in the value of fresh air and adequate ventilation and was to become an authoritative writer on the subject of fevers, saw to it that the design was in accord with medical needs, and the Infirmary became one of the best administered of the poor-law sickhouses of the Metropolis. The juxtaposition of workhouse and infirmary on a single site had many advantages also from the administrative point of view, although it was destined to become a source of embarrassment when, three-quarters of a century later, the policy of separation of the two types of institution had been adopted by the Government.

The positions of the buildings in their relationship to one another is admirably shown in Horwood's map of London, published between 1794 and 1799 *(p.12)*, which also includes the older premises to the north-east of the Burial Ground on the south-side of Paddington Street, which were then on the point of being demolished.

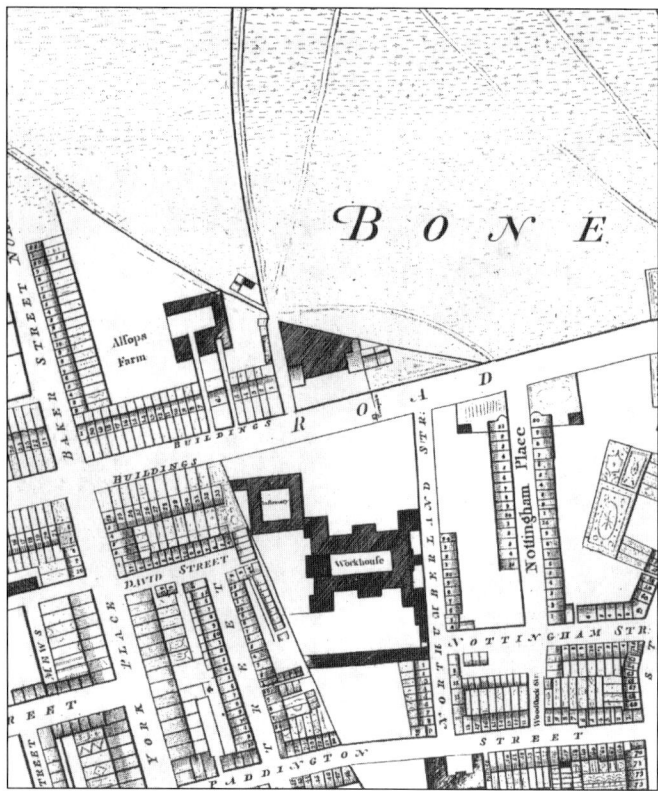

Horwood's Plan of 1794 showing the workhouse in Northumberland Street

Life in the Workhouse

The workhouse was designed as an all-purpose establishment in which paupers of every kind could receive the relief or treatment appropriate to their needs, and the term 'pauper' included not only those whose poverty arose from age, infirmity or economic distress, but also the sick, the lunatics, the mental defectives, the orphans and deserted children, the expectant and nursing mothers and the vagrants. From the start it was necessary to classify the applicants who sought relief and to allocate rooms and wards for each category of person taken into the Workhouse or the Infirmary. The Men's and Women's sides of the House were kept strictly separate and husbands and wives were parted immediately on admission. It was all the more essential to maintain a detailed system of classification as numbers grew. The far-reaching effect on economic conditions of the French War, which began in 1793 and lasted on and off until 1815, resulted, throughout the country, in widespread distress and, although the consequent increase in pauperism was greatest in rural areas, the resources of the Metropolitan parishes were also severely strained. By 1797 the number of inmates in the Workhouse and Infirmary at Marylebone had risen from the three hundred of 1776 to the remarkable total of 1,168. The Workhouse was, in fact, full and, much against their will, the Directors and Guardians, were compelled to grant out-relief in many instances in which they would have preferred to require entry into the House.

The Workhouse was, moreover, the administrative centre

PARISH of St. MARY-LE-BONNE, in the COUNTY of MIDDLESEX. APRIL 28, 1797.

ANY Persons willing to serve the WORKHOUSE of the said Parish with Mouse Buttocks, Clods, and Stickings of Beef, clear of bone, at per stone; Legs and Shins of Beef, in sets, not to weigh less than 50lb. at per set; Mutton, in carcases, the head and suet excepted, not weighing less than 9 stone, nor more than 11 stone, at per stone; Suet, at per stone; all kinds of Butcher's Meat for the Master's table, at per stone; Butter, at per cwt.; Gloucestershire and Wiltshire Cheese, at per cwt. Peas, Oatmeal, Small Beer, Milk, Groceries, Oil, Vinegar, Soap, Candles, Coffins, and Shrouds; also with the best Windsor, Pontop, or Tanfield Moor Coals, at per chaldron, Pool measure, to be delivered free of all expences, for one year from the 24th of June next; may attend the Board of Directors and Guardians of the Poor of the said Parish, to be held at the Workhouse, in Northumberland-street, Mary-le-bonne, on Friday, the 26th of May next, at 11 o'clock in the forenoon, and deliver their proposals, sealed up; in the mean time, may receive any necessary information, by applying at the said Workhouse. By order of the Directors and Guardians of the Poor, R. W. COCKMAN, Clerk.

Left: Account of work done in the workhouse, 1781

Above: Advertisement for supplying the workhouse with 'mouse buttocks', 1797 (These were small triangular pieces of meat behind the knees of cattle)

for the entire field of operations of the Directors and Guardians. Their board-room and offices were here and it was here also that the investigation of claims for outdoor relief was carried out and payments of such relief were made. In course of time, the staff of salaried officials grew into an organisation of some complexity.

The administration of the Workhouse was directed by the Master, who in 1799 commanded a salary of £60[6] a year in addition to board and lodging, and who was assisted by the Matron, who received £50[7] a year in addition to these emoluments. In the nineteenth century, it became the practice for a married couple to be selected for these two principal positions but, even where this was the case, there was frequent friction between the two. The spiritual needs of the paupers were provided for by the Chaplain, an appointment normally filled by a local clergyman in conjunction with his other duties. He conducted two services on Sundays, read prayers on Wednesdays and Fridays, administered the sacrament once a month, visited the wards regularly and, after the establishment of the schools within the Workhouse, examined the schoolchildren and supervised the work of the schoolmaster, the schoolmistress and the infants' schoolmistress. In 1799 he received £80[8] a year.

The poor who were not sick or infirm were expected to work, and to this end an officer with the ominous title of Taskmaster was employed. He was responsible for supervising the paupers at their work, which lasted from 6 am to 6 pm in the summer months and "as long as they could see" between 1 November and 1 March, with a half-hour break for breakfast and a one hour break for dinner. On Saturdays, work finished at 12 noon, except for those who had not completed their allotted quota. The Taskmaster received no fixed salary but was paid 2s[9] in the pound on the proceeds of all work done by the poor, except for needlework which was largely carried out by the women in the lying-in wards and so outside his province. In 1798 he received £151 19s 6d[10] under this arrangement, in addition to free board and lodging for himself and his family.

It can well be imagined that there was every incentive to oppression and the burden of work was very onerous. A return made in January 1799, when there were 882 inmates in the workhouse (not including the Infirmary), reveals that 417 were set to work and that, of these, 191 were engaged in spinning or in winding yarn or thread, 42 in knitting and plain work, seven as tailors, eight as shoemakers, five as carpenters, 20 as labourers, two in teaching the children, 21 as nurses, 27 as household servants and 94 in the picking of oakum or flock, a task reserved for the more recalcitrant cases. Not all these were, of course, under the supervision of the Taskmaster. Some were employed on the domestic work of the workhouse, for which pauper labour was expected to be fully utilised. In 1828 the figure of the Taskmaster disappears, a foreman or superintendent with a fixed salary becoming responsible for seeing that work was properly carried out.

In the Infirmary there were in 1799 a resident apothecary, a matron (or head nurse) and four paid nurses in addition to the pauper women who undertook nursing duties. A physician and a surgeon each received a gratuity of 100 guin-

Built in 1792 to the north west of the workhouse, the Infirmary was replaced by a new Hospital at Ladbroke Grove in 1881, and this building demolished in 1898; water colour, 1803

eas[11] to visit regularly and to examine and prescribe treatment for the inmates. The surgeon had permission to have one, and the apothecary two, pupils boarded and lodged at the workhouse.

To deal with applications for relief an Inspector was employed at a salary in 1799 of £100[12]. He it was who in the first instance examined applicants with a view to determining whether or not they had a legal 'settlement' in the parish or should be the subject of an application to the Justices for an order of removal to another. He was assisted by the Messenger, who executed orders of this kind and also warrants obtained by the Directors and Guardians from the Justices in poor law cases generally. He received a salary of £50[13] a year plus 7s 6d[14] per warrant for apprehending the fathers of illegitimate children chargeable to the parish. By 1847 the staff dealing with outdoor relief had grown to a salaried Assistant Overseer, two Superintending Inspectors, four Inspectors and a Messenger.

The inmates of the workhouse were subjected to a ruthless discipline, and severe punishments were imposed to enforce it. When, for example, the Master reported to the Rota Committee at its weekly meeting on Friday 19 July 1776 that Johanna Parry had "refused to perform such work as he had required her to do, such work being suitable to her strength and ability and had otherwise misbehaved herself", it was ordered that she should be punished by having a wooden log affixed to one of her legs, a punishment which regularly appears in the minutes for cases of this kind. At the next meeting seven days later, on hearing that she continued to be disobedient, the Committee ordered that "she be punished every day until Friday next by confinement in one of the sheds from the usual time of rising until the time of going to bed; that during the time of such punishment she be fed with a diet different from and more limited than that of the other poor and be not suffered to make use of snuff or any other unnecessary article". Ann Rollinson and Sarah Sanders, who had run away from the workhouse and sold a number of articles of their workhouse attire were, on their re-admittance in August 1790, ordered to be stripped naked from the waist upwards and whipped "until their backs shall be bloody" and then to be confined, set to hard labour and fed only on bread and water for a week. Cases of similar harsh punishments abound in the minutes of the Rota Committees.

The Master himself was, moreover, empowered to place in confinement for periods at his discretion any paupers who should "go out of the House without leave or refuse to work or be idle and not finish their task in time or refuse or neglect to obey the Master, Matron or Taskmaster's directions or pretend sickness or make any false excuse for not working or wilfully waste or spoil any stock or materials for work or wilfully do any other damage or profanely curse or swear or be guilty of drunkenness or any lewd discourse or any lewd or disorderly behaviour or absent themselves from prayers without just cause or waste the provisions or smoke tobacco in the bedchambers", subject only to his reporting the offences and punishments he had imposed to the Committee at weekly intervals.

The diet was rigidly prescribed. Breakfast at 8 am consisted of 'milk pottage' on Mondays and Fridays and water gruel on the remaining five days. For dinner at 1 pm the inmates received boiled beef on Sundays and Tuesdays and boiled mutton on Thursdays. The remaining days were 'meatless', pease soup being provided on Mondays and Fridays, butter (1 oz[15]) or cheese (2 oz) on Wednesdays and sweet dumplings on Saturdays. Supper, which was served at 6 pm in Winter and 7 pm in Summer, consisted of broth on Sundays, Tuesdays and Thursdays and butter or cheese on the remaining days. 4 oz of bread were allowed with every meal and special diets were permitted, where prescribed on medical grounds.

The paid officers ate at three tables, the Master's Table, the Kitchen Table and the Infirmary Table after the meals of the House had been completed, and enjoyed not only a more liberal diet but better quality food, a distinction in particular being drawn between 'Master's meat' and the meat served to the paupers. Even with the limited dietary laid down, the annual bill for provisioning the workhouse assumed colossal proportions. So far as meat alone was concerned, 5,922 stone[16] of beef, 7,128 stone of mutton, 1,399 stone of legs and shins and 1,714 stone of Master's meat were purchased in the year 1798. The total annual expenditure on the workhouse at this period exceeded £30,000[17], and the poor rate stood at 1s 11d[18] in the pound. The Directors kept a close watch on the quality of the goods supplied by the various contractors and did not hesitate to cancel contracts when the stipulated standards were not observed.

Young children, whose parents were not with them, were not retained in the workhouse but were boarded out with foster parents in the country within a month of admission until they attained the age of six years, an arrangement similar to that which had been made obligatory upon parishes within the Bills of Mortality under Hanway's Act of 1767, but was followed voluntarily in St Marylebone which was outside that area. In 1799, 293 orphans and deserted children were being maintained in this way at addresses in Ealing, Acton, Hammersmith and Kensington. At six years of age they returned to the workhouse, where they remained until in most instances they were apprenticed to a trade or sent into domestic service at some point between the ages of 12 and 16 years depending upon the demand at any given time.

Pauper lunatics were, moreover, not usually kept at the workhouse in cases where they were considered incurable but were sent to a private asylum maintained by one of the contractors, who at that period specialised in receiving paupers of unsound mind from the parishes of the Metropolis. Originally those from St Marylebone were sent to an establishment maintained by a Mr Stretton at Bethnal Green. Just before the turn of the century there were twelve men and nineteen women from the parish being maintained there. It is to the credit of the Directors and Guardians, who were of course an unpaid body, that they conscientiously visited from time to time the foster-homes of the younger children boarded out in the Middlesex countryside and also the private asylum at which the lunatics were cared for.

It was, however, not possible for them to know all that went on, and matters came to a head in 1826 when two of their number, Mr John Hall and the Reverend WI Birdwood, paid a visit to the White House, Bethnal Green where the St Marylebone cases were at that time being cared for by a Mr Warburton. In seeking one patient who could not be accounted for, they managed by their insistence to penetrate to an infirmary room to which they had not hitherto had access and saw at once evidence of overcrowding and cruelty. Lunatics were chained to the walls and, worst of all, although the room was only 18 ft long, it contained sixteen 'cribs' on which the 'wet' patients were made to sleep naked all night. At about the same time, the return to the workhouse of a patient, who had regained his senses and who told of occasions when he and his fellow patients had been chained to their cribs throughout the entire weekend, confirmed the Directors in their realisation that the place was wholly unsuitable. The lunatics were forthwith transferred to Sir Jonathan Miles' madhouse at Hoxton House.

The opening of the first county asylum at Hanwell in 1831 under the direct control of the Middlesex Justices provided in due course the answer to this difficult problem. Some classes of lunatics, particularly those awaiting certification or under observation, however, continued to be accommodated at the workhouse until shortly before the Second World War.

Another category of paupers, for whom provision had to be made and who were to provide a perennial problem, were the vagrants. The local Act empowered the Directors and Guardians to commit to the workhouse persons found wandering and begging or committing other acts of vagrancy

Lock-up, known as 'Jack Sheppard's Cage', where vagrants were imprisoned until 1813, after which it became part of the workshops at Marylebone Workhouse

and unable to give a good account of themselves and to detain them there on hard labour for not more than fourteen days, after which they were to be passed to their parishes of settlement. If male, they might, moreover, be whipped not more than three times for acts of misbehaviour during their stay. Vagrants and 'idle and disorderly persons', whose settlement was in the parish, could be detained in the workhouse and set to work until able to maintain themselves and to reimburse the Directors and Guardians the cost expended in maintaining them and their families. This latter provision operated very harshly until its repeal in 1815.

The designs for the workhouse included, as is indicated

in a minute of the Directors and Guardians dated 1 March 1776, prison cells which were presumably intended primarily for use in connection with vagrants. When the question of the demolition of these cells, which were contained in a separate one-storey block, arose in the last quarter of the nineteenth century, some comment upon their origins was made in the correspondence columns of the local press and references were made to a tradition that Jack Sheppard had once been incarcerated there. Despite some references to the block in official minutes at the time of its proposed demolition as the 'Marylebone Bridewell', there is, however, no evidence that the cells existed before the workhouse was built, and Jack Sheppard belongs to an earlier period.

One of the more colourful personalities who was reduced to becoming an inmate of the workhouse in these early days was Lieutenant John McCulloch, who died there on 27 December 1793 at the age of 77 years. He had served as Commissary Assistant of Stores to the garrison at Oswego in the American colonies in 1755, and, when taken prisoner there by the French the following year, had been taken to Quebec. Here he found an opportunity to make a survey of the rocks and fortifications above the town and was able to pass a report upon them to General Shirley. He returned to England under an exchange of prisoners in 1757 and was interviewed by General Wolfe, whose second and successful attempt to capture Quebec in 1759, which involved the scaling of the Heights of Abraham behind the city, is stated to have taken into account many points of detail derived from McCulloch's observations. In 1760 McCulloch was appointed a lieutenant in the marines and while serving on the *Richmond* under Captain Elphinston was responsible for the capture of the French man-of-war *Felicité*.

When he died in the workhouse, another war with France had just broken out. In 1797 a militia corps was formed in the parish, known as the St Marylebone Volunteers and nicknamed 'Bluebottles' on account of the distinctive colouring of their uniforms. The volunteers were given permission to keep their arms in the workhouse building and did so until they were disbanded in 1801 on the signing of the truce, which preceded the Peace of Amiens. The militia formed when hostilities broke out again a year or so later was on a new model and stored its arms elsewhere. Apart from this patriotic exception and a few occasions, when public meetings were permitted in suitable accommodation within its precincts, the use of the workhouse premises for other than their primary purpose was not encouraged. A suggestion by the balloonist Vincent Lunardi in 1786 that he might use the Women's Yard as a launching ground for a new manned 'aerostatic machine' to be filled by an entirely new method was refused, even though it was proposed that the workhouse should fix admission fees and retain all profits over and above Mr Lunardi's expenses of £180[19].

The Expansion of the Workhouse after 1815

The workhouse continued to grow. A small additional workshop block was erected in the Men's Yard in 1817, the Infirmary was expanded in 1825, and two years later additional buildings to house the boys' school were approved. 1841 saw the rebuilding of the women's workshops and the provision of additional dormitories to accommodate up to 200 more women, and in 1843 a new building for fifty able-bodied men was erected at the rear of the Chapel. These alterations had the effect of increasing the approved capacity of the workhouse to 1,449, made up of 152 aged and infirm men and 195 other men; 246 aged and infirm women, 35 nursing mothers and 426 other women; 188 boys and 111 girls over seven years of age; 61 infants between two and seven years old and 35 children under two years of age accommodated with their mothers in the nursery. The Infirmary continued to house 300 patients, so that the maximum approved capacity for the establishment as a whole was now 1,749.

Changes were also found necessary in the administration of the workhouse during this period. When Thomas Rein relinquished the post of Master in 1813 after twenty years in the position, great difficulty was experienced in finding a successor of sufficiently high calibre to manage the complex organisation which the House had now become. William Rockett was appointed but was found unsuitable within a matter of weeks, and his successor, William Hopwood, was dismissed after a similar short period. The post was then left vacant until 1815, the Clerk to the Directors and Guardians assuming responsibility for the Master's functions as well as his own during the interregnum. For the next three years the position was reinstated but matters were evidently considered far from satisfactory, for in 1818 the post of Master was abolished and a general re-organisation carried out, under which the Clerk was also designated General Superintendent and with the assistance of a Deputy Clerk assumed responsibility for all aspects of the administration, which was divided into eight departments.

The Superintendent's Department was responsible for the general management of the indoor poor, the paying and visiting of the outdoor poor, executing orders for removal, apprehensions, etc, and servicing meetings of the Directors and Guardians. The Steward's Department dealt with all questions of provisioning and stores. The Matron's Department ran the domestic economy of the House, the issuing and laundering of clothing and linen and the work of the kitchen, the nursery and the girls' school. The Medical Department was responsible for the care of the patients in the Infirmary and the needs of the outdoor sick. The Manufacturing Department was responsible for organising the work done by inmates and the disposal of the products of that work. The Boys' School was treated as an independent department and there were also the Accounts Department to deal with financial matters and the Clerk of the Works Department to maintain the fabric of the House and carry out day-to-day repair work. Spiritual ministration remained the special province of the Chaplain.

Under the re-organised arrangements the Master, Edward

Stiles, reverted to the subordinate position of Steward and his duties were strictly limited to those associated with that post. The Directors and Guardians may well have been influenced in these measures by the outstanding ability of their Clerk, Stephen Watts, who held the Clerkship from 1798 right up to his death at an advanced age in 1837, when he had served the Vestry in one post or another for 59 years.

The New Poor Law

The wave of radicalism, which in the 1830s ushered in the Age of Reform, extended the parliamentary franchise and purged the municipalities of corruption, brought in its train two statutes which were destined to shape the future of poor law administration in St Marylebone. The Vestries Act, 1831 (Hobhouse's Act) struck a severe blow at the whole concept of select vestries by substituting for them a vestry elected by the ratepayers wherever a prescribed majority of the ratepayers wished to make this reform. In St Marylebone, where the radical element known as the Barlow Street Committee (named after Little Barlow Street, now Cramer Street, where they met) had been in the thick of the fight for the passage of Hobhouse's Bill, the procedure laid down was at once invoked, and in 1832 the Select Vestry was replaced by a body of Vestrymen elected for a three-year term, one third retiring annually. The Act did not affect the number, functions or powers of the Directors and Guardians of the Poor, but it instituted a Board of five Auditors elected directly by the ratepayers at the annual elections, all five retiring each year.

In their early years the Auditors were dominated by the Barlow Street element and conceived it their duty not merely to audit the accounts but also to comment and make recommendations upon every aspect of the Vestry's administration, and this led to some friction with the Directors and Guardians when wholesale reforms of the workhouse and poor relief generally were suggested in the periodical audit reports.

In their report of October 1832 the auditors inveighed against the complexity of the workhouse administration in forceful words. "Upon taking a comprehensive review of the whole machinery of this large establishment", they said, "the Auditors have cause to the decided opinion that there are some radical defects in its constitution. It is an overgrown monster with many and powerful members but without a head to stimulate or direct their energies. Divided into seven or eight departments, each has its peculiar notions and technical arcana and is as independent and ignorant of its co-adjutant neighbour as if they were the antipodes of each other". A year later, a similar complaint is voiced, "The Workhouse is too large and complicated an establishment for the grasp of so fluctuating a body as the Directors and Guardians, as they at present arrange themselves, but yet the mighty machine moves onward. No single mind can encompass all the departments into which the establishment necessarily resolves itself during one year's service; nor is a numerous Board so competent to watch the practical details of business as a limited number". The Auditors went on to suggest that the Directors should appoint a large number of small committees to supervise aspects of the work, a recommendation which they chose to ignore completely.

21

In 1833 the Auditors also drew attention to the fact that the workhouse accounts had not been drawn up in the manner prescribed by the local Act of 1795, only to receive the quite remarkable reply signed by the Chairman of the Directors and Guardians, the Rev William Ilbert Birdwood, that "the Auditors must be aware that the present Board cannot be amenable for every foolish clause which may be introduced into an Act of Parliament." This must surely be a statement of independence without parallel in the history of relations between local authorities and the legislature.

In due course the reforming zeal of the Auditors waned, and by 1837 their comments were directed solely to the financial matters which were their real province. One result of their criticisms was, however, to give the many-membered monster back its head. In 1833 the post of Master was restored; the Steward, Isaac Twilley, being promoted to the position. Stephen Watts was now an old man content to confine his energies to the clerking of the Board meetings.

The other measure which was to affect the work of the Directors and Guardians was the famous Poor Law Amendment Act, 1834, which brought the old Elizabethan poor law to an end and replaced it with the austere New Poor Law based on Benthamite principles. Workhouses were henceforth to be forbidding places, 'less eligible' than the worst a poor man might encounter outside its walls. Outdoor relief was to be forbidden to able-bodied paupers wherever such a rule could be enforced, and where it could not, onerous labour tests were to be imposed to exclude all but the genuinely necessitous. Parishes were to be grouped into unions to provide viable areas of administration and each union was to be governed by an elected Board of Guardians.

More important still, the arrangements throughout the country were to be subjected to a rigid central control, three Poor Law Commissioners being appointed, who would with the aid of an inspectorate and a secretariat see to it that the 'principles of 1834' were maintained. Their powers to make Orders binding both on individual Boards of Guardians and on Boards generally covered not only questions of general administration but also points of detail and rendered them virtual dictators, for they were not responsible in Parliament in the way in which departments of the Central Government in general were. The Commissioners with their ruthless determination to restore economic stability after the vast expansion of expenditure on poor relief over the previous thirty-five years, soon acquired the nickname of the 'three bashaws' (ie pashas) 'of Somerset House'.

Friction with the Poor Law Commisioners and the Poor Law Board

It was fortunate for the Directors and Guardians that St Marylebone was not merged into one of the new unions but was left a 'separate parish', its size and financial resources being recognised as adequate for this purpose. Parishes whose arrangements for poor relief were governed by local Acts, moreover, continued to enjoy a limited measure of independence from central control. The Commissioners had no power to supersede a 'local Act' authority which proved refractory, and although the 1834 Act empowered them to issue regulations, rules and orders to such authorities on points of management and administration, they hesitated to do so, except where there was evidence of a serious abuse calling for rectification, and they certainly stopped short of imposing their views solely in the interests of standardisation. The Workhouse at Marylebone accordingly continued as before, but with the Directors and Guardians, jealous of their local Acts, ever on their guard and suspicious of the Commissioners, with whom a sort of "cold war" was waged. Requests from Somerset House for information on various internal matters were, as often as not, refused, and little co-operation was shown on proposed new departures.

In 1844 for example, a further Poor Law Amendment Act empowered the Commissioners to group parishes and unions in the metropolitan area into districts to provide 'district asylums' (ie casual wards) for vagrants and so deal with the problem of vagrancy in London in accordance with an overall plan. An order by the Commissioners the following year placed St Marylebone in the north-western asylum district for this purpose. The Directors and Guardians refused to co-operate in the plan, intimated that the workhouse could adequately cope with its own and declined to pay its quota of the asylum district's expenses, even though this was a clear statutory obligation. A similar attitude was adopted by several of the other parishes and the whole scheme for district asylums for vagrants collapsed. The Directors and Guardians were, however, alive to the problems to which the vast increase in vagrancy in the 'hungry forties' gave rise and in February 1846 opened two Nightly Asylums (one for males, one for females) entered from York Court, a narrow alleyway off East Street (as Chiltern Street was formerly called) which ran along part of the western boundary of the workhouse.

Here wayfarers and persons found wandering and destitute were admitted for one night only. Except when brought in by the police, they were required to seek admittance not later than 9 pm, the doors of the male and female asylums being opened at 6 pm and 5 pm respectively in the winter months and at 7 pm in the summer. Before having supper, they were examined, searched to ensure that they had no money to obtain a night's lodging elsewhere and thoroughly washed and cleansed. All knives and other dangerous instruments were required to be handed in on admittance and were handed back before discharge in the morning. Supper and breakfast each consisted of 8 oz of bread and a pint of gruel or soup. Vagrants were warned that any damage to property during their stay would result in their being given into custody and prosecuted and their particulars published in the *Police Gazette* for the information of other parishes. The Male Asylum consisted of two rooms, the lower one 65 ft by 11 ft 8 in and the upper one 56 ft by 12 ft. The Female Asylum comprised a single room 36 ft by 16 ft. About 60 males and 40 females could be accommodated each night and, in contrast to the views of the Poor Law Commissioners for such establishments, no task of labour was imposed, the Directors apparently taking the view that, with persons staying overnight only, it would be difficult to enforce one. In the first week of opening 148 vagrants passed through the asylums,

WORKHOUSE WOOING.

AIR—"There's nae luck about THE HOUSE."

Dedicated, without permission, to the Inhabitants of Mary-le-Bone.

Oh! have ye heard the news abroad,
  Come tell us what's about,
They say the saucy jade herself
  Has let the murder out.
How shall I open this affair,
  Since names I dare not mention,
And any thing beyond a joke,
  Is far from my intention.

CHORUS.

But it's all blown—the murder's out,
  Its talked of high and low,
How Tommy Dip, the tallow man,
  Got fond of Sally Snow.

(*Spoken.*)—Well its all about a pair of turtle doves the've been a long time hatching though it was a twelvemonth last Valentine's day they paired.

'Twas in the *Parkus* Mary Bone,
  This soft amour began,
The belle a tuckesome pauper was,
  The beau a Vestryman ;
My hero then if you would see,
  Who did this lady handle,
You'll just step into Crawford Street,
  And buy a tallow candle.
    Where its all blown, &c.

(*Spoken.*)—Aye, Tom had better stuck to the dripping, but the fat's in the fire now ; well 'twas *melting* moments and all in the way of business.

The fair she was the *turkus* pink,
  'Twas fair he should select her,
For Tom you know moreover was
  A Guardian and Director;
The damsel from Saint Lukes had come,
  And was the Member's sister,
Ah, Tom, the wily dog knew this,
  And that was why he kiss'd her.
    But its all blown, &c.

(*Spoken.*)—Oh, yes, here's your parish authorities for you, with the New Poor Law Bill, and its Bastardly Clause, Tom was working the Workhouse on a new system, called the self-supporting.

The courtship was no doubt good fun
  Just for the time it lasted,
But by this said illicit love,
  Tom's character got blasted;
His Brother Guardians shew'g'd the joke,
  The rumour got about,
They threatened Tom with Coventry,
  And turn'd his *romax* out.
    And 'twas all blown, &c.

(*Spoken.*)—Well, but what's the harm. A little innocent recreation between a Guardian & Pauper it's all human nature, as old Tom Beardley would say. How some'dver they made madam walk her chalks.

Tom followed her to Bayswater,
  And re-commenced the game,
And when they were caught in the act,
  She blow'd poor Tommy's name ;
When tax'd with her adultrous deeds,
  This little jade, rot her,
She blush'd and cried, upon my soul
  'Twas only Mr. ——
    Then 'twas all blown, &c.

(*Spoken.*)—Yes she regularly let the cat out of the bag then, and no mistake Tom's tail dropped between his legs, and he shook like a dog in a wet sack. But the landlady would'nt have it at no price and sings out—
  Don't talk to me you saucy jade
    Of Mr. Pot or Pan.

Why lius not he a wife at home?
  Sure he's nice young man ;
Tom promised them all sorts of things,
  Did on his knees beseech,
That she'd some little mercy shew,
  And would not go and peach.
    Then it was all blown, &c.

(*Spoken.*)—Sall had some misgivings and see't which way the wind was blowing, so

No mercy shew, exclaimed his pal,
  And straight this truth imparted,
Of all the pauper grinding crew,
  Tom is the hardest hearted.
Nay blow the truth in pity's cause,
  Cut short his reckless sway,
And thus cut short a long account,
  'Gainst Tom on judgment day.
    For it's all blown, &c.

(*Spoken.*)—Yes, when that day comes the poor will say Tom was too hard upon them, and ax where's their bread, but Sall will swear he was too soft upon *she* and and ax where's her *vartue.*

They vow'd Tom's rows were all moonshine,
  He came there for to good,
The base affair to undermine,
  They went to Underwood.
Tom streight was tax'd with his misdeeds,
  And offer'd no denial,
But bounc'd and swore an action he
  Would bring, and go to trial.
    But 'twas all blown, &c.

(*Spoken.*)—An action you know was all flummery, cause the thing was as clear as the daylight.

Proceedings long were entered on,
  Tom mean time loosing leather,
And when the trial should have come off,
  Tom sported the white feather.
His spouse has taken him in tow,
  And swears no more he'll roam,
For after dusk he shan't be seen,
  A hundred yards from home.

(*Spoken.*)—No ! No ! A joke's a joke, but there's a tight rein put on him now, and the rugus gas will be put in the lock-up when he's abroad.

I now must bid this pair adieu,
  And leave them to their fates,
Just hoping Tom's propensitive
  Won't tend to raise the rates.
But Vestrymen they look so blue,
  I fear there is some ground
To think they mean to clap it on,
  Just four-pence in the pound.
    But it's all blown, &c.

(*Spoken.*)—Four-pence, that's heavy ! What, Tom have all the fun, and the parish pay the piper? But they say that some one else stopped the defendant's mouth, and Tom (that is the parish) stood the racket of this score only.

Then take a hint ye rate-payers,
  Some tramps in office fix,
And thus in future you'll prevent
  Such gallivanting tricks.
When next you're call'd on to elect,
  Choose steady men and moral,
Your Workhouse should a Workhouse be,
  And not a common brothel !
    CHORUS.

For it's all blown—the murder's out,
  'Twill very soon be found,
Tom cut these capers to the tune
  Of four-pence in the pound.

This ballad 'dedicated, without permission, to the inhabitants of Mary-le-bone', commemorates a local scandal involving one of the Guardians and a workhouse inmate, c1840

but by the following year the weekly total had jumped to 920. Within a very short time, however, an outbreak of fever caused them to be closed and they were not re-opened.

Friction with the Commissioners came to a head in 1846 when a coroner's jury at the inquest on the body of Louisa Mordaunt, in returning a verdict of death "from the want of the common necessaries of life", added a rider regretting "that the officers of the parish of St Marylebone had not used sufficient diligence in scrutinising the necessities of the deceased person". The Home Secretary requested the Poor Law Commissioners to carry out a full inquiry into the matter and also into a similar case which had recently occurred in St Pancras, and they used the occasion to examine not only the arrangements for the relief of the outdoor poor, which had been called in question, but also the entire field of poor law administration in the two parishes. Whilst the Assistant Overseer and Inspectors were exonerated from blame for the death of Louisa Mordaunt, attention was drawn to other irregularities. In particular the Directors and Guardians were as obstructive as possible in connection with the inquiry, refusing to produce original documents until forced to do so and instructing the officers who had been ordered to give evidence to do so only if permitted to have the questions and answers written down.

The workhouse now entered on what was probably the darkest period of its history. In the latter half of 1846 it became so overcrowded that adequate standards of management were impossible to maintain. This arose very largely from an Act, passed that year, amending the law of settlement in such a way as to render persons with five years' residence in a parish who applied for relief irremovable to another parish. The primary intention was to call a halt to the wholesale removal of Irishmen back to Ireland, for this was the year of the failure of the Irish potato crop, when to send men back to Ireland was to condemn them to certain starvation. St Marylebone had a considerable Irish colony, whose members could now claim poor relief without fear of removal, and in the last six months of 1846 the number of inmates in the workhouse and infirmary rose by about 500. There was, moreover, no prospect of any early change in the situation. The highest number ever accommodated on one day was 2,264, when every ward was crowded and the workshops were pressed into service as additional dormitories. Although the position stabilised a little after the first influx, the total number of inmates continued at a level little short of 2,000.

Overcrowding and the consequent increase in expenditure brought with it a drive for economy and the Directors and Guardians found themselves in the unhappy position of being under fire from two fronts – from the ratepayers who resented the increased call upon their purses on the one hand, and from such Chartist bodies as the Poor Man's Guardian Society, who were quick to draw attention to any defect in administration, on the other. Various internal economies were effected. The widespread practice of paying small gratuities of varying amounts to pauper inmates who assisted in the domestic work of the house, amounting in total to £843 11s 11d[20] during the year 1845, was regulated from 1846 by new rules limiting both the amount of these payments and the numbers of persons who received them. One shilling[21] a week and no more was to be paid to 53 who acted as nurses, 20 laundrywomen, two blind men who taught the schoolchildren singing, one man who lit and extinguished the gas lamps, one driver and horsekeeper, one cutter-out, three personal assistants to the Master, Matron and Clerk, four pauper bearers and two chairmen. Two shillings[22] a week was to be paid to the cook and the barber and one shilling and sixpence[23] a week to a pauper who taught handwriting in the girls' school and the woman who laid out the dead. A man named Butler, who acted as porter at the cross-door between the Workhouse and Infirmary, recording transfers between the two establishments and ensuring that no such movements took place without the proper written authorities and who received gratuities amounting to £16[24] a year, was ordered to be discharged as a pauper and taken onto the salaried staff of the workhouse. These measures effected a saving of over £500[25] in the annual expenditure on gratuities. A more strict accounting procedure for stores and a re-examination of the diet scales also served to bring about some economy.

The desire for economy could, however, descend to petty levels. In the minutes of the meeting of the Directors and Guardians on 16 December 1853 we find a report by the "Committee appointed to consider the subject of providing plum puddings to the inmates of the workhouse on Christmas Day". The Committee recommended that the practice of giving plum pudding at Christmas should be discontinued as it "had an injurious effect, being an inducement to many to endeavour to obtain admittance into the workhouse" or, alternatively, if the Board should not accept this view, that each pauper should be limited to an 8 oz [26] portion. To the lasting credit of the Directors, the inmates received their Christmas pudding, as they had done each year since the workhouse opened, although the restriction to half-a-pound per inmate was agreed to. An amendment that "usual quality raisins" should be substituted for currants was also passed. Even with the limitations imposed, the 1853 puddings contained 350 lb[27] of flour, 280 lb of fruit, 150 lb of suet, 50 lb of sugar and 6½ lb of spice.

In 1856 there was a further brush with the central authority. The Poor Law Commissioners had been replaced in 1847 by a Poor Law Board, having at its head a minister responsible to Parliament and the Board was perhaps in a stronger position than its unpopular predecessor to deal with recalcitrant Guardians. The 'cold war' however had continued. On 25 July 1856 Mr Broughton, the Marylebone Police Court magistrate, drew the attention of the Directors and Guardians to allegations against the Master of the Workhouse, Richard Ryan, by two young women brought before him for creating a disturbance in the Refractory Women's Ward at the workhouse. They alleged that they had been brought to court only because they had no marks of ill-treatment and that other girls named Howard, Sullivan and Edmunds all aged between 17 and 19 years had been cruelly beaten by the Master and the Porters with canes in their attempts to quell the disturbance. Medical evidence proved the allegations to be true, and this was the more serious as an Act of Parliament strictly forbade the corporal chastisement of females in workhouses. The Directors and Guardians after some consideration decided against the dismissal of the officers concerned, but resolved that "considering the extreme provocation they received, the Board are of the opinion that the merits of the case will be met by the officers in question being reprimanded by the Board and told that, should the like occur again, instant dismissal will be the consequence".

In view of the public outcry which followed, the Poor Law Board ordered one of its inspectors to hold an inquiry, after which they called upon the Directors and Guardians to dismiss the Master. (The two porters had resigned already). The Directors refused to alter their earlier decision and something like a stalemate ensued in which the Poor Law Board took the strange step of sending a letter direct to Ryan calling upon him to resign. After further acrimonious correspondence, the Directors with some reluctance accepted the resignation. The departure of Ryan was celebrated in a street ballad entitled "The Women-Flogger's Lament of Marylebone Workhouse", a copy of which has survived at the City of Westminster Archives Centre.

This incident was used by the Poor Law Board as a pretext to issue a regulatory order for the St Marylebone Workhouse in October 1856. Although the Directors sought counsel's opinion whether this action under the Act of 1834 was legal, they appear to have submitted to it. The "refractory women", mainly hardened young women of abandoned character and abusive language, had long been a problem at the workhouse. The Directors had made it their concern to keep this class of pauper quite separate from the other women inmates, and

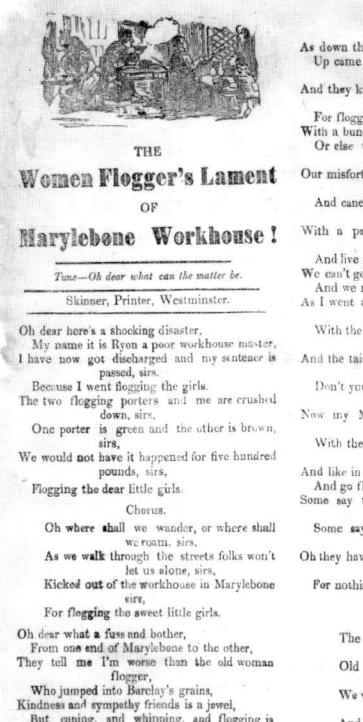

This satirical ballad is dedicated to Ryan, the master of Marylebone Workhouse, who was removed from office in 1856 for flogging female inmates

Members of the United Cooks' Society preparing a monster plum pudding at Marylebone Workhouse for the Lancashire operatives (Illustrated London News, 1863)

Poor labourers were at the mercy of agricultural failures and trade fluctuations, caused partly by wars. This picture shows an attempt to relieve the poverty of the Lancashire cotton workers whose supply had been cut off by the American Civil War.

particularly from the young girls leaving the school and returning to the workhouse in between periods of domestic service, who were accommodated in a special building known as "the Cottage". As far back as 1832 a riot on the part of the refractory women had resulted in sixty panes of glass being broken and the unrepentant ringleader, Anne Boyd, on that occasion assured the magistrate that prison was preferable to the treatment she received at the workhouse, and that she would behave ten thousand times worse when she returned there at the end of her sentence.

More friction with the Poor Law Board arose over the Directors' insistence in 1857 to exclude one of the Board's inspectors from one of their meetings and over the determination of the Board to extend the system of district audit to the parishes with "local Act" poor law functions. The Poor Law Board took a stern line in these matters, bringing a test case in the High Court against the Vestry of the neighbouring parish of St Pancras, whose Directors and Guardians had adopted a similar line on the question of district audit and had also refused the Board's inspector permission to take measurements of parts of their workhouse in the course of his duties. When the Bench pronounced in favour of the central authority the battle was virtually over. The independent vestries, including St Marylebone, began to submit to regulation from the centre with as good a grace as possible.

The Removal of the Schools

The overcrowding which prevailed in the St Marylebone Workhouse after 1846 cried out for action, and one solution which early suggested itself was the removal of one class of pauper, ie the school-children, to new premises. Such a step was in accord with the policy of the Poor Law Board which had in 1844 and 1848 obtained statutory powers to create 'school districts', which were groupings of parishes and unions to provide by a pooling of resources, large residential schools in country districts at which pauper children could be brought up away from the workhouse atmosphere.

St Marylebone did not wish to join hands with other parishes in this way, but the idea of providing its own 'separate school' in an outlying district held certain attractions, and as early as 1849 we find the Directors and Guardians agreeing to this proposal in principle and recommending it to the Vestry, who, of course, were responsible for matters affecting land and property.

The boys' school, girls' school and, since the cessation of the boarding out of the 'under-sixes', the infants' school, provided, within the workhouse, a basic education which, for the period, was of a not unreasonable standard. The Timetables of the Boys' and Girls' Schools which catered for children between 7 and 16 years of age were as follows:-

Boys' School		Girls' School	
6.00-7.00	Rise, make beds, prayers, clean shoes and wash	6.00-8.00	Rise, make beds clean shoes, wash. Prayers and religious instruction
7.00-7.45	Gymnastic exercises, (Saturdays excepted)		
7.45-9.00	Prayers, breakfast. Play	8.00-9.00	Breakfast. Recreation
9.00-10.00	Historical reading, with explanations	9.00-11.30	Reading. Spelling tables and arithmetic
10.00-11.00	General and mental arithmetic, tables, use of clock dial for learning the time of day		
11.00-12.00	Grammar. Parsing and Dictation	11.30-12.30	Working in copy books. Dictation
12.00-2.00	Dinner. Recreation	12.30-2.00	Dinner. Recreation
2.00-3.00	Writing in copy books and arithmetic	2.00-5.00	Needlework, knitting, learning the time of day and domestic employment
3.00-4.00	Reading with explanations		
4.00-5.00	Geography with maps		
		5.00-6.00	Supper. Recreation
6.00	Supper	6.00-8.00	Needlework, knitting and domestic employment
8.00	Prayers. Retire to bed	8.00	Prayers. Retire to bed

Wednesday and Saturday forenoons were devoted in both schools to Scripture reading and examination of previous lessons. Wednesday afternoon was a half-holiday on which in fine weather the children of both sexes were taken into Regent's Park. Saturday afternoon was also a half-holiday for the boys, but the girls were expected to engage in washing, cleaning, the mending of their clothes and stockings and preparation for Sunday. The timetable of the Infants' School, which comprised children from two to seven years of age, was more fluid, but two to three hours a day were expected to be spent in reading, spelling and tables. After 1848 a limited number of children were regularly maintained at Mr Weekly's Metropolitan Establishment at Margate, a private institution which contracted with several of the London poor law authorities.

The workhouse atmosphere powerfully affected the minds of the young ones, and, as a report of 1849 pointed out, children brought up there felt no sense of shame in re-entering its walls in adolescent or adult life. Between 1840 and 1849, 326 girls had left the school for domestic service (other than apprentices) and of these 89 were known to be leading abandoned lives, and a further 20 had had illegitimate children who had subsequently become chargeable to the parish. Of 137 boys who had left the school to go to sea in the merchant service between 1843 and 1847, 83 returned to the workhouse and again became chargeable. The apprentices, on the other hand, and those joining the Services generally proved more satisfactory. A school in the country would remove the atmosphere of pauperism from the start and would also allow industrial training to be included in the curriculum and so provide a preparation for that battle of life, in which the adult paupers at the workhouse had been so cruelly defeated.

There were long delays, however, in obtaining the Vestry's approval in determining whether the local Acts permitted the Directors to do what they intended and, above all, in finding a suitable site. Eventually a large school was built at Southall in 1860 and the schoolchildren transferred to it. It remained in being until July 1916, when it was taken over as a military hospital by the Australian Forces. Thereafter the Guardians joined the Kensington and Chelsea School District, which maintained a large residential school at Banstead (still in existence but re-christened 'Beechholme') and a branch school for younger children at Marlesford Lodge, Hammersmith (now known as 'Palingswick House' and used for housing by community organisations). After some demur, which was only overcome by correspondence from Cardinal Manning, it was agreed that Roman Catholic children should be sent, not to the Parochial School at Southall, but to orphanages and residential schools maintained by Catholic bodies at North Hyde (Southall), Walthamstow and later, certain other localities.

After 1860 the children kept at the workhouse itself were confined to the very youngest with their mothers in the nursery, the foundlings and deserted babies until of an age to go to Southall and a few older children in transit. The workhouse from its earliest days had its regular trickle of foundlings brought in by the watch or the police or even left on its own doorstep, sometimes with those pathetic notes which still characterise such cases today. In 1815 an infant left in this way at the workhouse gate had the following doggerel verse pinned to its clothing:-

"I am little Kitty, my parents are poor.
I crave your pity, now I am left at your door.
I do not despair but a hope I do cherish
I shall be taken care of, as I am left to the parish."

The practice of giving foundlings names based on the place where they were found was, it is pleasing to record, exercised with increasing discretion as time progressed. The early days of the workhouse saw several innocent waifs condemned to go through life bearing names like Cavendish Square.

New Casual Wards

The 1860s brought a number of changes in Metropolitan poor law administration, due to the increasing determination of the Poor Law Board to deal with the problems of the Metropolis on an overall basis. The Metropolitan Houseless Poor Act, 1864 made a renewed attempt to deal with vagrancy; not this time by the formation of asylum districts, but by requiring each union and separate parish to provide satisfactory casual wards for destitute wayfarers, wanderers and foundlings, the cost being reimbursed by the Metropolitan Board of Works. The Act was a temporary one, effective from 29 September 1864 to 25 March 1865, but was made permanent in 1865, and in 1867 the financial responsibility

A drawing of Marylebone workhouse by W A Delamotte, one of the inmates in 1866 before many of the buildings were reconstructed

of the Metropolitan Board of Works was transferred to the newly formed Metropolitan Common Poor Fund. The vagrant wards at the St Marylebone Workhouse were approved for the purposes of the Act and had a capacity for 25 men, 30 women and 10 children each night. In accordance with the instructions of the Poor Law Board, they were designed along particularly austere lines, the beds in the men's ward consisting of mattresses on raised wooden platforms, each 6 ft 10 in by 2 ft 3 in, separated by dwarf planking, and those in the women's ward of coir or flock mattresses on iron bedsteads. Two rugs were provided for each 'casual' plus, in the case of

The eastern end of the chapel yard, pencil drawing by W A Delamotte, a workhouse inmate, 1866

The western end of the chapel yard, with the Chapel in the centre; pencil drawing by W A Delamotte, a workhouse inmate, 1866

New ward for the casual poor at Marylebone Workhouse, Illustrated London News, 28 Sep 1867

Grim though it might appear to us, the new casual ward for vagrants at Marylebone Workhouse was hailed as an exemplary model. This picture shows the sleeping bunks which pivoted so that the floor could be easily cleaned. Most workhouses underwent extensions and improvements in the 19th century to relieve the problem of overcrowding

the women, one blanket. Each of the wards was heated by a single stove and lit by gas all night. Supper consisted of bread only (6 oz[28] per man, 5 oz per woman and 4 oz per child). Breakfast was made up of a like quantity of bread with a pint of gruel in the case of adults, and half a pint of gruel in the case of children.

During the six months experimental period before the Act became permanent 4,749 casuals (1,861 men, 2,282 women and 606 children) passed through the wards, an average of 25 per night, and only 37 were refused admission (28 for refusing to bath, seven for being in possession of money above one shilling[29] and therefore able to secure a night's lodging elsewhere, and two who objected to the hardness of the beds). The largest number of admissions took place on 14 November 1864 which, as the Master grimly remarked in his report, was the night following the public execution of the murderer, Franz Muller, outside Newgate Prison. The 'casuals' were required to pick 2 lb[30] of oakum before leaving, but the Act did not permit their detention for more than four hours after breakfast if this task had not been completed. Later legislation in 1871 and 1882 made conditions harsher, making the task of work more strenuous and rendering it illegal for a casual pauper to discharge himself before 9 am on the second day following his admission, or before he had completed his task of work. This period was, moreover, extended to 9 am on the fourth day in the case of a casual pauper admitted to any London casual ward more than once during one month. The Guardians were, however, empowered to relax these conditions in the case of bona fide seekers for work.

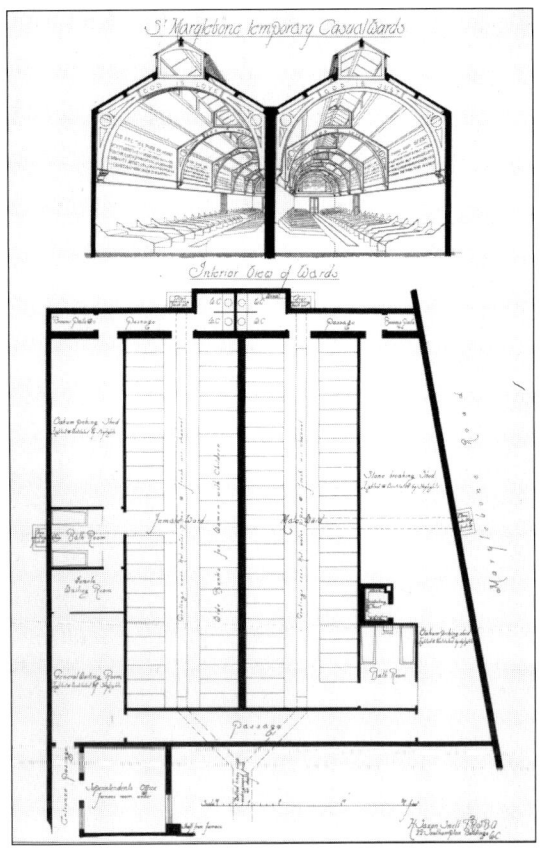

Plan of the temporary casual wards, Northumberland Street, erected in 1867

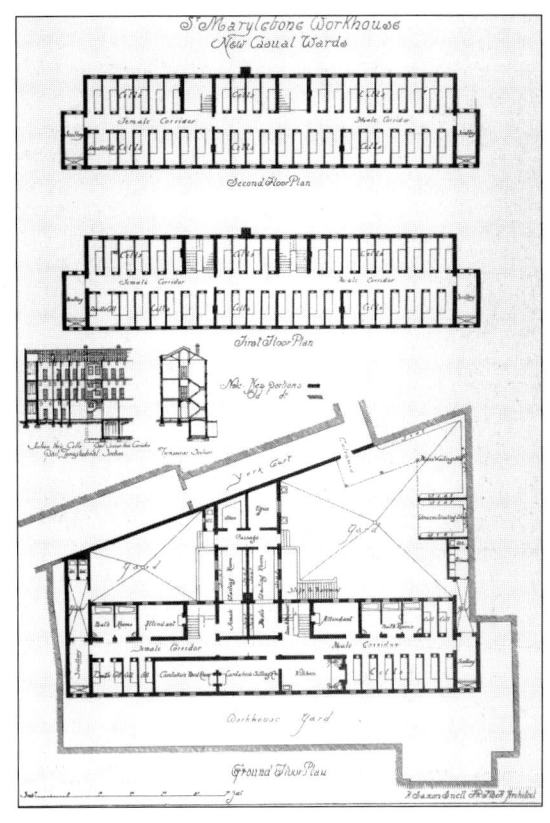

Plan of the new casual wards, David Street, Baker Street, published in 1881; no provision is made for stone breaking, all the inmates being employed in picking oakum

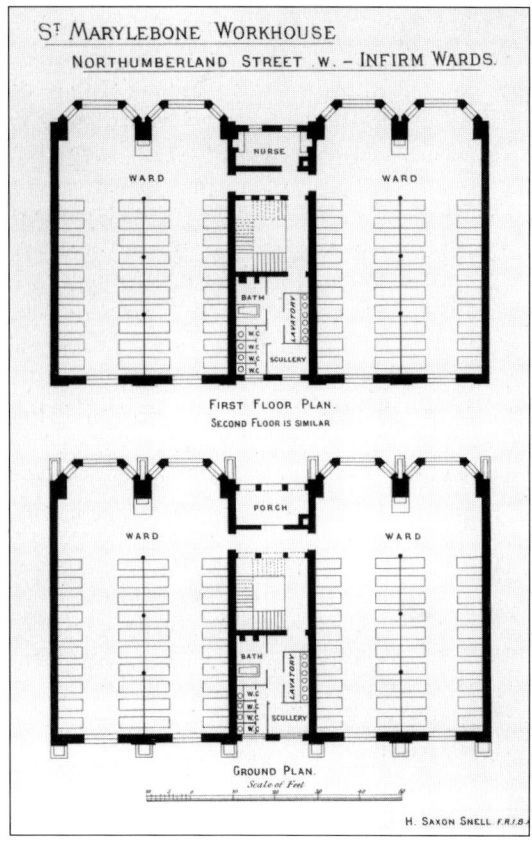

Plan of the Infirm Wards at St Marylebone Workhouse, Northumberland Street, erected in 1867

In 1867 the Directors and Guardians erected new temporary casual wards in the portion of the workhouse at the corner of Marylebone Road and Northumberland Street. A sketch of their interior and a plan of their layout appears in *Charitable and Parochial Establishments* by their architect, H Saxon Snell, and it is seen that a religious atmosphere was added to the austerity of the wards, for the Scriptural texts, painted in large letters upon the walls, included not only the exhortation to turn from criminal ways found in Ephesians 4 v 28, but also the warnings as to moral conduct embodied in Colossians 3 v 5. The only means of entrance to, and exit from, the perimeter enclosing the casual wards and their associated bathrooms, disinfecting rooms, oakum-picking sheds and stone-breaking shed was by way of a narrow passage past the strategically placed superintendent's room.

The Metropolitan Poor Act, 1867 brought into being the Metropolitan Asylums Board, which took over from the individual poor law authorities in London the task of providing mental hospitals and hospitals for small-pox and other infectious diseases, and was later to acquire, as additional functions, the maintenance of a training ship for pauper children, the provision of remand homes for children awaiting, trial and ultimately the provision of casual wards for vagrants. Hitherto the Directors and Guardians had sent Marylebone smallpox cases to the Smallpox Hospital at Highgate, paying the fees charged by that independent institution. When, however, epidemics occurred and all patients could not be admitted there, they were forced back on their own resources. In the epidemic, which lasted from May 1863 to February

1864, a building at the workhouse housing the men's Oakum Ward and a dormitory above it, which was separated by a yard from the remainder of the workhouse, were pressed into service as a smallpox hospital. The nurses were strictly confined to the building and a man was posted at the yard gate communicating with the rest of the workhouse to prevent any movement in or out. All food and stores were passed through him. Patients were admitted and discharged by an entrance from York Court. Infected clothing and bedding were buried in two deep pits in the yard after being covered with layers of lime and disinfecting powder. 215 patients were admitted during the nine months, of whom 22 died. When a further epidemic occurred in the last weeks of 1866, an iron building at the Vestry's Stone Yard at Lisson Grove was used as a temporary hospital. The Stone Yard, used in connection with road construction and repairs, was situated at the end of Capland Street and occupied the extensive site between Richmond Street (now Orchardson Street) and the Regent's Canal, today filled by a particularly ugly electricity generating station built in 1905. This is now the site of a Westminster City Council depot and Social Services building.

The Act of 1867 set up also the Metropolitan Common Poor Fund, which made certain aspects of poor law administration (whether transferred to the Metropolitan Asylums Board or not) a common charge upon all the authorities in the Metropolis, thus effecting a form of 'rate equalisation'. These changes could not, it was felt, be efficiently brought about whilst the authorities in the Metropolis looked to differing statutory foundations for their existence and functions.

The Act accordingly empowered the Poor Law Board by order to supersede the local Acts and to bring all Boards of Guardians in London under the provisions of the Poor Law Amendment Act, 1834. The Board was not slow in exercising these powers, and with effect from 2 August 1867 the Directors and Guardians of the Poor of the parish of St Marylebone ceased to exist. The Board of Guardians which replaced them was elected in accordance with the arrangements in force generally throughout the country, had no dependence upon the Vestry and was subject from the start to the detailed regulation and control of the central authority.

The St Marylebone Board of Guardians

With these changes in administrative organisation and the internal re-allocation of accommodation following the removal of the schools to Southall, the workhouse entered upon a calmer period. The Master, George Edward Douglas, who had been appointed to this responsible office in 1862 at the early age of thirty one, proved, moreover, to be a man of superior calibre to the succession of incumbents who had preceded him in the post. He had already served as Storekeeper and Master's Clerk and knew the workhouse and its ways thoroughly. He was to remain Master for 32 years, a period of service unequalled by any other holder of the office at St Marylebone before or since, and his reports over these years show him clearly to have possessed that correct blending of firmness and humanity called for at a time when social attitudes to poverty were undergoing a transition to more enlightened standards. He used his position to relax some of the harsher aspects of the workhouse regime. "At least twenty years ago" he was to write in a report on the work of the House during the year 1892, "I quietly permitted the old women to have a private teapot and make their own tea, conditionally that it was done at the one time, four o'clock, and that both the pot and tea were supplied by friends". He adds the understanding comment, "A cup of tea is a wonderful comfort to an old woman who, in the ordinary way, would have to wait until the evening meal at 6 for it".

His ability to handle a difficult situation was demonstrated on the occasion of the Regent's Park ice disaster on 15 January 1867. Happening to be walking in the park with his wife, who was the Matron of the Workhouse, he was present when the ice gave way and some two hundred skaters found themselves struggling in the waters of the lake. He immediately persuaded the police officers to commandeer vehicles to take persons rescued and suffering from shock to the nearby workhouse, which he placed at their disposal for this purpose. He then hurried back to make the necessary arrangements for their reception and treatment by the medical staff of the Infirmary. There can be little doubt that his prompt action saved the lives of several of the skaters. The bodies of the forty victims of the disaster were also brought to the workhouse.

The Rebuilding of the Workhouse and the Removal of the Infirmary

The most pressing problems facing the new Board of Guardians concerned the structural condition of the buildings comprising the workhouse and infirmary. Early in 1867 part of the wall of one of the female infirm wards in the workhouse fell down into the yard during the night, fortunately without injury to the inmates, who were in bed at the time. As a result the Directors and Guardians had approved the rebuilding of a complete section of this part of the premises (the southern end of the portion abutting on Northumberland Street) 104 ft long and 65 ft wide, to a new three-storey plan by Mr H Saxon Snell, the architect who designed the temporary casual wards erected in the same year, to which reference has already been made, as well as many other poor law buildings in London and elsewhere. Shortly after this part of a stone staircase on the north side of the chapel collapsed, and it was found necessary to shore it up from top to bottom. The time had clearly come to contemplate the large-scale reconstruction of the premises as a whole. The fact that the leases had only twenty-three years to run, however, militated against a large capital expenditure of this kind, and negotiations were accordingly entered into with the Portland and Portman estates, resulting in the substitution of new leases of eighty years duration in 1870. A special Workhouse Reconstruction Committee was then appointed to investigate the complete replacement of the older parts of the premises.

The ranges of buildings along Northumberland Street were

the first to receive attention. After the clearing of the existing blocks, the new female infirm wards erected in 1867 were continued northwards in a similar style of architecture to form a three-storey block 190 ft in total length. A new block of the same design and height some 150 ft in length and also used for infirm female inmates was erected and connected to it by an archway, which provided the main entrance to the workhouse and incorporated small receiving wards and a porter's lodge. The remainder of the Northumberland Street frontage up to its junction with Marylebone Road was filled by a new single-storey block to house the Guardians' offices and board room and the Registrar's Office. All this work was carried out in the years 1875 and 1876, and on 4 November 1878 a new three-storey casual ward block was opened in the middle section abutting on the western boundary of the site, the temporary casual wards nearer to Northumberland Street having been pulled down. The new ones were quite different in character from the old. The open wards with their platform beds separated by low wooden planks and their large-lettered Bible texts on the walls were not reproduced. Instead each 'casual' was provided with a tiny individual cell, differing from a prison cell only in having no lock. The new casual wards were kept quite distinct from the remainder of the workhouse, being entered only from York Court. Some years later, when the erection of Portman Mansions and the extension of East Street (now Chiltern Street) through to Marylebone Road had resulted in the disappearance of York Court, a new narrow roadway was formed from Marylebone Road to provide access to the casual wards and to keep them a distinct entity.

It was at this period that provision was first made for services for the Roman Catholic inmates to be held within the workhouse, in place of special facilities to attend the local churches. The first service was taken by Rev J Guiron of the Spanish Place Chapel in January 1877 in a small chapel formed by the screened-off end of a needle-room in one of the women's blocks, before an altar presented by Cardinal Manning, 194 persons being present. A larger and more suitable chapel was later provided in the Women's Infirm Block in Northumberland Street and used until in LCC days the Catholic chapel was moved to the Central Administrative Block.

The Workhouse Reconstruction Committee devoted a great deal of its attention to the future of the Infirmary. A report in 1866 by Dr E Smith, medical officer to the Poor Law Board, and Mr E Farnall, one of the Board's inspectors, on the condition of the workhouse infirmaries in the Metropolis was by no means as unfavourable to St Marylebone as to many other authorities. It had, however, become the Board's policy to press for infirmaries to be kept, wherever possible, separate from workhouses and to form 'sick asylum districts' covering several unions, where necessary, to provide a viable catchment area for a large infirmary. There was no suggestion that St Marylebone should form part of such a district, but the Board brought pressure to bear on the Guardians to remove their infirmary to a new locality as part of the reconstruction in contemplation. There was the more incentive to do so as the number of inmates in the workhouse was again on the increase. In 1876 a site was found at Rackham

Street, Ladbroke Grove, and a fine hospital (now known as St Charles Hospital) was in due course built there and opened by the Prince and Princess of Wales on 29 June 1881. The architect, Mr H Saxon Snell, received a letter of praise for its design from Miss Florence Nightingale, which has been preserved in the Wellcome Historical Medical Museum in Euston Road. The removal of the sick from the infirmary at the workhouse released a considerable amount of accommodation for general use. The workhouse continued, however, to maintain lunatic and idiot wards for the small number of pauper patients under observation or awaiting certification and removal to the County asylums or the hospitals of the Metropolitan Asylums Board. In addition maternity cases continued to be received at the workhouse, the labour and lying-in wards having for many years been in the workhouse and not the infirmary portion of the premises. A large number of the latter cases were of unmarried mothers who had nowhere else to turn. In the year 1892, for which fully analysed statistics are available, 187 confinements took place at the workhouse, of which 147 were of unmarried women, the youngest being fifteen years of age. With four of the unmarried cases, it was the mother's fourth child, with 13 the third and with 34 the second. 109 of the unmarried mothers were servants by occupation.

Although the Workhouse Reconstruction Committee was discontinued shortly after the new Infirmary at Ladbroke Grove was completed, further building works were carried out in the succeeding years. In 1887 a new laundry block was erected along the southern boundary, to replace an older

View of corridor in the workhouse showing the door leading into the entrance hall; watercolour by J P Emslie, 1898

View of the workhouse courtyard; watercolour by J P Emslie, 1898

block which had become dangerously dilapidated. In the same year a new experiment was initiated by the erection of a small two-storey block to house ten aged married couples, thus breaking down, to some limited extent at least, the rule hitherto rigidly enforced that husband and wife must be separated on admission. In 1888 a five-storey block for 240 able-bodied women was built at the south-west corner. Another acquisition occurred when it was decided in 1886 that the disused burial grounds on either side of Paddington Street should be laid out for other purposes. That on the south side became a public park, but that on the north side was, by arrangement with the Vestry, made over for the exclusive use of the workhouse inmates as an 'airing yard', to use the term then employed for a recreation and exercise yard.

The effect of the rebuilding operations which had taken place was to transform completely the outward aspect of the establishment. The new blocks were all large and unmistakably 'institutional' in design. Those which they replaced had been almost entirely of two-storey construction, with the extra buildings which had been added over the years fitted in in piecemeal fashion. The character of the old workhouse is skilfully portrayed in an engraving, made by an inmate ('W.A.D.') in 1866, of the courtyard and buildings in the north-east corner of the establishment and included as an illustration in *Charitable and Parochial Establishments* by the architect, H Saxon Snell, who comments that the artist was a member of a famous artistic family who had fallen upon reduced circumstances. This clue does not suffice to make possible a positive identification, but it may be mentioned that the inmates included a certain William Alfred Delamotte, who was in the workhouse for several months in 1866 before being transferred to the Islington Workhouse, and who might perhaps have been a member of the famous family of engravers and artists bearing his surname.

The Able Bodied Poor

In the last quarter of the century an attempt was made to reduce the number of able-bodied applicants for relief, or rather of that element among them which in a shiftless manner used the workhouse as a means of subsistence without making very great efforts to live independently outside its walls. The practice had long obtained of applying a test to able-bodied applicants for outdoor relief and the Directors and Guardians had adopted the policy of sending male applicants of this kind to work at the Stone Yard in Lisson Grove on the onerous task of breaking stones for a small wage. Failing this the workhouse test was applied, outdoor relief being refused and the persons being required to enter the House. A type of individual had, however, sprung up who was content to accept 'the offer of the House' but once in created a problem by discharging himself at frequent intervals and returning within a day or so. Cases even occurred in which, immediately upon being voluntarily discharged, a man called upon a relieving officer for a re-admission order which, however, he did not present at the House until a late hour at night after having avoided the work and discipline of the establishment for the day.

In 1872 the Local Government Board tried to deal with this problem by creating a special test workhouse for able-bodied paupers in the Metropolis, and the Poplar Workhouse was chosen for this purpose, after it had transferred its sick to a district sick asylum, its children to a district school and its aged and infirm to the workhouse of another union. At Poplar the discipline was made more rigid, the diet more restricted and the daily work task of oakum-picking or stone-breaking more onerous than at any other workhouse. St Marylebone joined in the scheme to the extent of giving able-bodied applicants for relief the 'offer of Poplar', wherever there seemed any doubt as to the genuineness of the case. The experiment foundered when in 1878 a Police Court magistrate refused to convict a woman accused of unwillingness to do her quota of oakum picking at Poplar on the ground that such work was not a fit task to set women in receipt of Poor Law relief. It was thereafter not possible to maintain the harsh regime, and in 1881 the Poplar Workhouse reverted to its normal use. A similar experiment was pursued a little later under which the Kensington Workhouse was made a test workhouse for able-bodied male paupers, and St Marylebone joined in the scheme from 1889 on. Once again, however, it was scarcely successful. Some hardened paupers discharged themselves and were re-admitted as frequently at Kensington as they had been in their home area. The Master, in one of his reports mentions two St Marylebone paupers ('A.S.' and 'J.R.') who, between January 1891 and December 1892, had been discharged and re-admitted at Kensington 116 and 104 times respectively. The Kensington scheme was finally dropped in 1905.

Throughout this period the workhouse continued to be a place at which all capable of it were expected to work. Apart from those domestic tasks which served the needs of the House itself, many of the male inmates were kept employed in cutting wood into suitable lengths with crank-operated circular saws and chopping up the resultant logs into firewood, which was sold to a contractor. In the year 1892, 645,325 bundles of wood, 467 sacks of chips and 308 sacks of sawdust were sold in this way for £1,028 11s 4d. The women in the same year cut out 10,181 garments and items of table and bed linen for use in the House and also made up 8,685 similar articles for an outside firm.

Further Rebuilding

After the removal of the infirmary cases to Ladbroke Grove in 1881 the population of the workhouse remained fairly constantly in the region of 1,600. In the middle of the last decade of the century the Guardians felt that the time had come to complete the reconstruction of the premises, and in 1895 the Local Government Board approved an overall plan whereby all the remaining buildings built before 1867 were to be demolished and replaced. The architect entrusted with the design of the new blocks was Alfred Saxon Snell, FRIBA, a son and partner of the designer of the portions of the workhouse erected after 1867, and his plans envisaged three new ranges of buildings, ie a central block separated by courtyards from the existing and proposed blocks on the perimeter of the site, a range of two communicating five-storey

Demolition of the old workhouse in progress, 1898; water colour by J P Emslie

blocks parallel to, but set back somewhat from, Marylebone Road and a two-storey block for able-bodied men on the west side of the site, between the existing casual ward block and the projected Marylebone Road block. To enable work to proceed, the disused Holborn Workhouse at Gray's Inn Road was leased by the Guardians, and some 400 beds were maintained there between January 1896 and April 1900 as an 'overflow' workhouse.

The foundation stone of the central block was laid on 19 May 1897 and it was opened by the Bishop of London on 20 May 1898. The centre section of its main (eastern) frontage was of two storeys, the ground floor being primarily devoted to administration, the Master's and Matron's offices etc, and the upper storey being occupied by the Main Chapel. An octagonal belfry surmounted the building and the clock and bells from the demolished block were transferred to it. A large stone bearing the inscription 'ST MARYLEBONE WORKHOUSE FOR THE POOR BEING LAME IMPOTENT OLD AND BLIND ERECTED IN THE YEAR MDCCLXXV', taken from the old workhouse entrance, was also built into the northern wall of the block.

Behind this front section and partially separated from it by light wells lay the large single-storey kitchen, in which the meals for the entire establishment were prepared and behind this again the even larger dining hall, 120 ft by 50 ft, in which they were eaten. The bakery was situated immediately below the kitchen, with which it was connected by a bread lift. The preparation of food for so large a number of people called for special equipment and the new kitchen contained nine coppers, six of 200 gallons and three of 100 gallons capacity, two 50 gallon beef-tea boilers, three copper tea boilers, a 200 gallon tea infuser and a double set of potato steamers with a total capacity of three quarters of a ton, as well as three very large gas ovens, three smaller ones, a gas grill and steam-heated cutting-up tables and plate-warmers. The northern and southern sections of the central block were of three storeys and were used as wards for the semi-chronically sick and more seriously infirm inmates and others requiring special medical attention; the northern wing for males in this category and the southern wing for females and young children, with a maternity wing on the second floor.

The five-storey Marylebone Road blocks were designed primarily for the aged and infirm male inmates but also included at the extreme ends of the ground floor the mental observation wards for both sexes with associated day rooms and padded cells; the Alexandra Ward for men being at the western end and the Dorcas ward for women being at the eastern end. The foundation stone of these blocks was laid on 31 October 1898, and they were opened on 21 March 1900. In accordance with a practice fashionable at the time, a florin, a shilling, a penny, copies of the *Times*, the local newspapers, the order of proceedings for the day's ceremony and a statement concerning the Diamond Jubilee celebrations of the previous year were placed in a container in a cavity within the foundation stone when it was laid, for the benefit of posterity. A similar procedure had been followed with the Central Block in 1897. Certain of these items were recovered when the blocks were demolished in 1965. The Able-Bodied Men's Block, finished in 1901, completed the reconstruction of the establishment.

Men in the dining hall of Marylebone workhouse in 1902.
From George R Sims (ed), Living London, vol II (I), p104

Casuals waiting for admission. From George R Sims, Living London, vol. II, section I, p106

The Break-up of the Poor Law

The approved capacity of the workhouse as rebuilt was fixed at 1,921 inmates. Initially this provided a substantial margin over and above the actual population of the House, but the first years of the twentieth century saw a rise in the number of inmates, and from 1903 to 1910 the establishment was once again virtually full. The forces which were to result in the break-up of the poor law were, however, already in motion. The Royal Commission on the Poor Laws and Relief of Distress sat from 1905 to 1909, and both the Majority and Minority Reports which issued from its work recommended the transfer of the functions of the Boards of Guardians to the councils of counties and county boroughs. As is well known the Minority Report went further, recommending that the functions, which the Guardians had come to exercise in regard to health, mental health, maternity and child care, should in future be dealt with within statutory frameworks appropriate to those spheres, rather than under the poor law, and was destined in the long run to have the greater effect.

The commencement of a scheme of old age pensions in 1908, the establishment of labour exchanges in 1909 and the initiation of compulsory insurance against sickness and unemployment in 1911 resulted in a decrease in applications for relief and in admissions to workhouses. During 1911 the number of inmates at the St Marylebone Workhouse fell by over two hundred to 1,689, and by the end of 1914 it had dropped further to 1,443. In 1912, moreover, new arrangements were made in regard to London's casual wards, for the Metropolitan Casual Paupers Order of the preceding year transferred the entire responsibility for this class of pauper from the individual Boards of Guardians to the Metropolitan Asylums Board. The Board took over from 1 April 1912 those casual wards which had been maintained in separate premises from the workhouse or which, like that of St Marylebone, had separate entrances and sufficient structural separation from the rest of the workhouse buildings to enable them to be treated as distinct entities.

The Board, however, found almost immediately that the twenty-four casual wards it acquired in this way were more than ample to meet the needs of an integrated service, and by the end of 1913 it had reduced the number to twelve, the St Marylebone casual ward block (now having the separate address of 29 Marylebone Road) being handed back to the Guardians on 1 August 1913. It had an interesting subsequent history, for from 22 October 1914 to 16 December 1915 it was used to house Belgian war refugees, and from 2 July 1918 to 10 May 1921 it was taken over as a military detention barracks. On its return to the Guardians on 16 April 1922 it was decided to carry out extensive internal and some external alterations and convert it into a central outdoor relief station. It was opened as such by the Mayor of St Marylebone on 25 July 1923 and continued in use until 1948, when responsibility for outdoor relief passed from the London County Council to the National Assistance Board and the block again became available for other purposes.

The First World War brought some other changes to the St Marylebone Workhouse. The numbers of St Marylebone inmates continued to fall throughout the war years, until by the end of 1918 they numbered only 658. Several other unions were, however, in difficulties, as their institutions had been taken over by the authorities as military hospitals, and hastened to enter into agreements with St Marylebone to accommodate numbers of their paupers on their behalf. In this way some 400 beds were filled by inmates from Paddington and lesser numbers from Hampstead, Hammersmith and Lewisham, and the total population of the workhouse remained between 1,000 and 1,200. The advent of peace, moreover, brought little change in this position for it had already become apparent that the days of the existing poor law authorities were numbered, and the Boards of Guardians were in several instances reluctant to resume control of their former premises and quite happy to continue the war-time agreements indefinitely. The Maclean Committee on Local Government had reported to the Ministry of Reconstruction in 1918 recommending the transfer of poor law functions to county councils and county borough councils, and the House of Commons passed a resolution in May 1925 accepting this re-organisation in principle, so that throughout this period there was little doubt what the end would be. The Local Government Act, 1929 finally accomplished the transfer which had been inevitable ever since the Royal Commission report of 1909, and on 1 April 1930 the London County Council took over the functions of the Metropolitan Asylums Board and of the 25 Boards of Guardians and four poor law school districts situated in its area. At the St Marylebone Institution at this time there were 1,131 inmates, consisting of 577 St Marylebone cases, 327 Paddington cases, 98 Hampstead cases and 129 cases from eleven other unions.

The London County Council

The objectives which the London County Council set itself with regard to the institutions and homes for which it now became responsible were firstly, to remove from the ambit of the poor law those categories of inmates which could be catered for under health or education powers, secondly, to break down the 'general mixed institution', so that each establishment, so far as possible, would deal with one class of need only, and thirdly, as a more ultimate aim, to work towards establishments of a size most appropriate to the class of need filled. The unified control which the Council possessed over the institutions of the former authorities throughout the County facilitated specialisation of the type envisaged, but the size of the problem and the fact that the early years were dominated by a severe financial crisis rendered it inevitable that progress would have to be spread over a considerable period.

The St Marylebone Institution, as the workhouse was now called, came at once under the direction of the Council's Public Assistance Committee. The small single-storey block at the corner of Northumberland Street and Marylebone Road housing the Guardians' offices became an Area Office of the Public Assistance Department for some years, and when no longer required for this purpose, was used by the Council for a District Surveyor's office.

Proposals for the complete re-organisation of the institution in accordance with the new policies were embodied in a three-year plan adopted in 1936, which fixed its approved

The old workhouse, built in 1878, as depicted in the programme to mark the opening of the New Central Relief Station in 1923 (see opposite)

The New Central Relief Station, converted from the old workhouse building, as pictured in the programme to commemorate its opening on 25 July 1923

maximum level of accommodation under the revised standards now in force at 1,543 beds (924 men and 619 women). The maternity ward was, in accordance with this plan, closed in November 1936 as soon as the opening of a new ward at Hammersmith Hospital had made such a step possible, and the two mental observation wards were discontinued at the end of August 1937. The nursery, which housed children too young to be sent to residential schools, was due to be closed by the end of March 1939, but an outbreak of infectious disease rendered it necessary to retain it for several months more, and it disappeared when the children were evacuated on the outbreak of war. Over these years, moreover, the institution gradually lost the 'able-bodied' element among its male inmates, for persons in that category were now being sent to the Sutton Training Centre, the Dunton Farm Colony and certain designated institutions only. A limited number of able-bodied women continued to be accommodated at St Marylebone. The effect of all these changes was to render the institution almost entirely a home for the aged and infirm.

The Second World War brought special problems to an institution with a population of over a thousand mainly elderly people in the centre of London. As a protection against enemy action the topmost floors of the taller blocks were taken out of use, and the number of inmates from 1940 to the end of hostilities was reduced to a level of between six and seven hundred. The institution in fact suffered air raid damage on some six occasions, the first being on 8 September 1940, when extensive blast damage from a bomb which fell on nearby Chiltern Court caused slight injuries to 31 inmates and five staff and the death of one aged inmate from shock, and rendered it necessary to transfer large numbers to other institutions. Nine nights later a delayed action bomb struck one of the Luxborough Street blocks and penetrated through to a needle-room on the ground floor, without casualties, but again causing the evacuation of the affected portion of the premises. On the night of 17/18 October 1940, five persons were slightly injured when the laundry and women's infirm wards sustained damage and the public mortuary, which adjoined the institution and had been used by it, was destroyed. Further damage was occasioned when a bomb exploded in mid-air immediately above one of the blocks on 25 October 1940. Minor incidents involving incendiary bombs also occurred on 24 September and 8 December 1940. For part of the war period portions of the second and third floors of one of the Marylebone Road blocks were taken over by the St Marylebone Borough Council as a recreation centre for civil defence workers.

Advent of the Welfare State

The end of the war saw the institution occupied to a level well below its capacity and the opportunity was taken to utilise parts of it for special tasks. For several months in 1947, for example, 250 beds in one of the Marylebone Road blocks were made available as a transit centre for displaced persons from the Continent coming to this country to undertake industrial and domestic employment. Two parties each 250 strong were received each week in this way, and the number of persons accommodated and fed during their brief stay was thus very considerable. A more serious task brought about by post-war conditions was the provision of accommodation for homeless families whilst awaiting re-housing or admission to the already overcrowded rest centres. Up to the middle of 1953, when other institutions took over this work, the wives and children of a number of persons rendered homeless were maintained in the south-western block formerly used for able-bodied women, thus enabling each family to remain as a unit until some steps towards re-housing could be taken, usually after a matter of a few weeks. Finally until December 1953, when a special hostel for them was opened in Great Guildford Street, Southwark, a small unit was maintained at St Marylebone for women 'casuals' or, as they became under the changed terminology of the social legislation of 1948, 'persons without a settled way of living'.

Apart from these special cases, however, the inmates were all in the category of aged and infirm persons, and within a few years of the end of the war their numbers had regained the pre-war level of between 1,100 and 1,200. The National Assistance Act, 1948 brought about considerable changes in their position and treatment. The poor law framework in which they had been dealt with hitherto was abolished altogether and the stigma of pauperism was removed. Henceforth the duty laid upon the Council towards them was to provide residential accommodation "for persons who by reason of age, infirmity or other circumstances are in need of care and attention which is not otherwise available to them". They were no longer to be treated as paupers seeking relief, but as persons to whom the community owed a special duty, and, to remove the element of charity so much detested under the poor law regime, residents in the homes were to pay a charge for their accommodation, after first receiving the retirement pensions which were their entitlement as of right under the National Insurance Act, 1946. The charge thus made was in normal circumstances to be calculated in such a way that a prescribed portion of the pension (now 16s[31] a week) was left to the individual as pocket money, enabling him to retain some measure of independence. The Act represented, therefore, not merely a continuation of the process of liberalisation and relaxation of restrictions which had proceeded progressively since 1930 or earlier, but a complete change in the basis of administration.

In keeping with the new arrangements an effort was made to remove the vestiges of stigma remaining from the old order. Institutions (or 'large homes' as they now became) were renamed in 1949, and the St Marylebone Institution became 'Luxborough Lodge', a name derived of course from

Luxborough Street, as Northumberland Street had been re-designated ten years earlier. The following year the term 'Warden' was substituted for 'Master', which still bore workhouse connotations, and simultaneously the various inscriptions and notices at the premises which used the older terminology were re-cast or obliterated.

Extensive maintenance works were, moreover, carried out. The kitchen was modernised and re-equipped, new boilers were installed which were later converted to oil firing, new lifts were installed in various parts of the home, the narrow archways at the main entrance were removed to provide a more suitable approach, a small modern two-storey block of staff quarters was erected at the northern end of Luxborough Street and the old relief station underwent a further transformation to become partly staff quarters and partly a self-contained small home for the aged, incorporating some accommodation for married couples on the lines of the small-sized homes, which the Council was now building in increasing numbers elsewhere. More importantly perhaps, the furnishings and fittings throughout the premises were replaced by others in keeping with modern fashions. A canteen, opened in 1940 in the former Able-Bodied Men's Block, provided a range of items on which pocket money could be spent, and the recreational facilities and library built up over the years continued to grow. Television sets made their appearance in many of the day rooms. Over the years, moreover, the diet scales had been made both larger and more flexible. At the height of the war, when foodstuffs were in short supply, an egg a week was allowed to each inmate and sweet puddings were provided every day from a date in 1943 instead of on four days a week. In the post-war period the dietary was further improved so that it fell little short of that enjoyed by the populace at large. Visiting facilities were extended so that visitors could be received each day instead of on two days a week. Residents were allowed to leave the precincts without formality. In these and many other less tangible ways the intentions underlying the 'welfare state' legislation were made a reality.

It is not easy for the historian to detail the innumerable changes which occurred at this time, but in the aggregate they represented a complete revolution in the social life of the home. The canteen and the library became the focal points for new activities in which the tremendous capacity for many-sided service of such voluntary organisations as the British Red Cross and the Women's Voluntary Services was given full play.

Weekly club evenings were held, seaside holidays were arranged, and concerts, outings and film shows were organised on a scale hitherto unprecedented.

For all this, it was abundantly clear that an establishment still housing over a thousand old folk was altogether too large to provide a homely atmosphere, and the old buildings, for all the adaptation that had taken place, could not disguise their institutional character which contrasted so strikingly with the modern architecture of the new small homes for fifty to a hundred residents erected since 1948. The results of the advances in the medical study of institutional neurosis over the previous quarter of a century also served to underline the need for a much smaller community as the basic unit of organisation. In 1962 the Council adopted a ten-year programme for the development of its Health and Welfare services, which amongst other proposals dealt with the future of the remaining nine "large homes". Three of them were considered suitable for retention, primarily for the most seriously infirm and semi-chronically sick old people needing a great deal of personal attention, subject to a continued policy of improvement to bring the buildings up to modern standards. The remaining six should, it was decided, be replaced over a period as capital expenditure programmes permitted, Luxborough Lodge being the first to disappear. To replace the accommodation lost by the closure of Luxborough Lodge, the building of fourteen new small homes in various localities, having capacities between 60 and 120 beds was put in hand.

Over the closing months of 1964 the inmates were gradually dispersed, many to the newly-built homes, but many also to the remaining large homes which shared something of its own atmosphere, good and bad. Planners dealing with human material always find a diverse response to their efforts, and there was not wanting an element among the old people of Luxborough Lodge which preferred the old and familiar to the new and strange and looked askance at the wear and tear of re-adjustment which the latter would demand. Some also with chronic ailments or seriously infirm were transferred to large, rather than small, homes in view of their need for specialised care.

In a fully developed welfare state the answer to the latter type of case may well prove to be a vast increase in geriatric units within the National Health Service framework, but in the meantime the large welfare homes provide the best available alternative and in this particular respect if in no other, have some advantages over the smaller and newer homes. At all events some proportion of the former inmates of Luxborough Lodge are now finding in such establishments as King's Mead (the old Chelsea Workhouse) an environment not unfamiliar to them.

The formal closing of Luxborough Lodge took place on 6 January 1965 at a function attended by the Mayor of St Marylebone, by Mr Quintin Hogg and by representatives of several of the voluntary organisations which had been associated with its work.

Later in the same year the buildings were demolished and the site cleared.

Upon the northern and western sections of the site of Luxborough Lodge it is proposed to erect a college of architecture and advanced building technologies with an associated hall of residence and a school of management studies, both of which will be associated with the Regent Street Polytechnic and will doubtless play an important role with the polytechnic, if and when colleges of advanced technology are elevated to university status. The southern part of the site is reserved for a twenty-one-storey housing scheme. These projects will cost in all just over three million pounds.

The story of Luxborough Lodge thus moves to its end. Before closing this account, however, it is fitting to recall the high standard of service and devotion which has been displayed by its past and present staffs, and the excellent work which has also been undertaken by the various voluntary organisations who have added their help to make life easier for the old people in the home. It is gratifying to record that, in the New Year's Honours List in 1957, Her Majesty the Queen was graciously pleased to appoint the Warden, Mr W Arblaster, MC to be a member of the Most Excellent Order of the British Empire (Civil Division), and that a similar honour was conferred four years later upon the Matron, Mrs E Underwood. Voluntary organisations which have played their part in providing additional comforts for the inmates range from the London Flower Mission, whose ladies last century paid weekly visits to distribute flowers to each ward and the Sunflower Negro Minstrels, who in the 1890s amused the inmates with their own particular kind of entertainment, to the more recent and more comprehensive work of the Brabazon Society, the British Red Cross, the Women's Voluntary Services, the Metropolitan Society for the Blind and the St Marylebone Old People's Committee.

In April 1965 the health and welfare functions of the London County Council, by virtue of the London Government Act, 1963, passed to the new inner-London borough councils and the question of the implementation or otherwise of the ten-year development programme worked out in 1962 now rests with the individual authorities who have taken up the reins. Much more remains to be done, but the action taken by the London County Council in regard to Luxborough Lodge will, it is hoped, serve to point the way ahead.

Endnotes

[1] £11.31 This and subsequent footnotes give the 2001 purchasing power equivalent to the sum in the text. Similar footnotes show metric equivalents of imperial weights.
[2] £2.54
[3] 85p
[4] £2.46m
[5] £1.363m
[6] £3,353
[7] £2,794
[8] £4,246
[9] £5.31
[10] £8,014
[11] £5,838
[12] £5,307
[13] £2,794
[14] £19.90
[15] 30g, 60g and 110g respectively
[16] Approximately 37, 45, 9 and 11 tonnes respectively
[17] £1.592m
[18] £5.09
[19] £1,139
[20] £47,360
[21] £2.72
[22] £5.43
[23] £4.08
[24] £869
[25] £28,252
[26] 225g
[27] 160kg, 125kg, 67kg, 22kg and 3kg respectively
[28] 165g, 140g and 110g respectively
[29] £2.34
[30] 900g
[31] £20.63

Appendix A
Diet tables in force at St Marylebone Workhouse in 1846

(See overleaf for Appendix B)

Afterword

by Brenda Weeden, University Archivist

In his final paragraphs on the closure of Luxborough Lodge, Alan Neate referred briefly to the plan to build a college of architecture and advanced building technologies on the northern and western sections of the site. The need for such a college had been identified in the Woodbine-Parish report presented to the London County Council in 1957. After some debate about where the proposed college was to be sited and how it was to be managed, in 1959 it was decided to place it on the Luxborough Lodge site as part of an ambitious scheme for the expansion of Regent Street Polytechnic.

London County Council had been supporting the London polytechnics since 1891. Regent Street was the oldest and largest of these, and had provided the model on which the others were founded. It originated in the philanthropic work of Quintin Hogg, the grandfather and namesake of the late Lord Hailsham who performed the closing ceremony at Luxborough Lodge in 1965. Hogg pioneered the provision of technical and vocational courses for young working men and women. In 1882 his Institute moved from the slums of Covent Garden to 309 Regent Street, a building formerly occupied by the Royal Polytechnic Institution – and the name polytechnic soon transferred from the building to the new model of educational institution which it housed. *(cont. p61)*

The rear of Luxborough Lodge before 1965

Luxborough Lodge from Marylebone Road before 1965

University of Westminster, Marylebone Road site: architect's model c1970

Architecture and construction were among the earliest Polytechnic courses, having been taught since the 1870s. After the Second World War, there was a great demand for professional and technical training from those whose education had been interrupted, and the School of Architecture was frustrated in its hopes of expansion by limitations upon space. So when the London County Council first approached the Polytechnic Governors with the plan to expand onto the Luxborough Lodge site on Marylebone Road, the suggestion was met with enthusiasm. In fact the plan was part of a wider one to transform Regent Street into a federal college. As well as the College of Advanced Architecture and Building Technology (CAABT) and School of Management at Marylebone Road, there was also to be a School of Engineering and Science on another new site in New Cavendish Street.

The LCC finally approved the reorganisation scheme in October 1962, and the Council's own Architects Department was appointed for the Marylebone buildings. The design was based around a central podium, and special features included the construction hall to act as a testing laboratory for large structures. Progress was slow. Demolition of the Luxborough Lodge buidings began in July 1965, and the site was finally handed to the contractors (Taylor Woodrow Construction Company) in December 1966. The new buildings were completed in February 1970, and came into full use the following September when Architecture, Building, Civil Engineering, Surveying and Town Planning moved onto the site. There was a separate block for Management Studies, and a tower block of student residences.

Both new buildings – at Marylebone Road and New Cavendish Street – were opened on 21 May 1971 by Lord Hailsham of St Marylebone, grandson of the founder, who was Lord Chancellor from 1970-1974. During the same ceremony, he also presented the institution with the Designation Parchment marking its change of name to the Polytechnic of Central London (PCL).

The new name resulted from changes in national policy in higher education. PCL was one of 30 polytechnics formed in 1970 as part of what was described as the public sector of the binary system of higher education, awarding degrees from the Council for National Academic Awards. The binary line was abolished in 1992, when PCL became the University of Westminster. During its first ten years, the University has invested over £75 million on the improvement and renewal of its buildings. The Marylebone Campus, currently housing the School of Architecture and the Built Environment and Westminster Business School, has undergone a £14.1 million refurbishment, providing new lecture theatres, an improved library and refectory, and a new entrance onto Marylebone Road. The refurbished buildings were officially reopened on 9 October 2002 by the Right Honourable Dame Mary Hogg QC, daughter of Lord Hailsham and great grand-daughter of the founder, who is a governor of the University.

Index

Numbers in bold type refer to illustrations

ACTON, 17
Acts of Parliament: Poor Relief Act (Knatchbull's Act, 1722), 6; St Marylebone Select Vestry Act (1768), 8; St Marylebone (relief of the poor) Act (1775), 9; St Marylebone Vestry Act (1795), 9; The Vestries Act (Hobhouse's Act, 1831), 21; Poor Law Amendment Act (1834), 22, 23, 37; Poor Law Amendment Act (1844), 23; Metropolitan Houseless Poor Act (1864), 31; Metropolitan Poor Act (1867), 36; Local Government Act (1929), 49; National Insurance Act (1946), 53; National Assistance Act (1948), 53; London Government Act (1963), 56
Arblaster, William (Workhouse Master, then Warden), 56, 57
Ashbridge Collection, 5

BAKER STREET, **35**
Ballads, **24**, 27, **27**
Banstead (location of Kensington and Chelsea District School), 30
Barlow Street Committee, 21
Barlow, W (Workhouse Master), 57
Barnett, James (Workhouse Master), 57
Beechholme (formerly Kensington and Chelsea District School at Banstead), 30
Bethnal Green, 17, 18
Bible, 30, 36, 39
Birdwood, Rev William Ilbert (Chairman of the Directors and Guardians of the Poor), 18, 22

Board of Guardians, 22, 37, (see also St Marylebone Workhouse: Administrative bodies: Board of Guardians)
Boyd, Anne (inmate), 28
Brabazon Society, 56
Bridewell, 6, 19
Bristol Workhouse, 6
Broughton, Mr, 26
Brown, William (Workhouse Master), 57
Butler (male inmate), 26

CAPLAND STREET, 37
Casual wards, 31, 34, 36, 48 (see also St Marylebone Workhouse: Buildings and wards)
Cavendish Square, 6, 31
Chelsea Workhouse (later King's Mead), 55
Chiltern Court, 52
Chiltern Street (formerly East Street), 23, 39
City of Westminster Archives Centre, 5, 27
Connor, Thomas (Workhouse Master), 57
Cooper, Charles (Workhouse Master), 57
Covent Garden, 58
Cramer Street (formerly Little Barlow Street), 21

DAVID STREET, **35**
Delamotte, William Alfred, **31**, **32**, **33**, 42 (see also W.A.D.)
Douglas, George Edward (Workhouse Master), 37, 57
Dunton Farm Colony (Sutton Training Centre), 52

EALING, 17
East Street (now Chiltern Street), 23, 39
Edmunds (female inmate), 26
Elizabeth II, 56
Emslie, JP, **40**, **41**, **44**

Euston Road, 40

FARNALL, Mr E (Board Inspector), 39

GALLUP, George (Workhouse Master), 57
Golden Lion (public house), 6
Grays Inn Road, 45
Great Guildford Street, 53
Greater London Council, 5
Guiron, Rev J, 39

HALL, John (Director of St Marylebone Workhouse), 18
Hammersmith, 17, 30, 49, 52
Hammersmith Hospital, 52
Hampstead, 49
Hampstead Workhouse, 49
Hanover Square, 8
Hanwell (location of lunatics' county asylum), 18
Harley, Mr, 9
Hattersley, George (Workhouse Master), 57
Highgate, 36
Hogg, Mary QC, 61
Hogg, Quintin (1845-1903), 58, 61
Hogg, Quintin, Lord Hailsham (1907-2001), 55, 58, 61
Holborn Workhouse, 45
Hopwood, William (Workhouse Master), 20, 57
Howard (female inmate), 26
Hoxton House, 18

IRELAND, 25
Islington, 8, 42
Islington Workhouse, 42

JALLINGS, John (Workhouse Master), 57

Jones, James (Workhouse Master), 57

KENSINGTON, 17, 30, 43
Kensington and Chelsea School District, 30
Kensington Workhouse, 43

LADBROKE GROVE INFIRMARY, see St Marylebone Workhouse: Ladbroke Grove Infirmary
Lancashire operatives, **28**
Lewisham, 49
Lewisham Workhouse, 49
Linton, Philip Newsam (Warden of Luxborough Lodge), 57
Lisson Grove, 37, 42
Little Barlow Street (now Cramer Street), 21
Local Government Board, 43
London County Council (LCC), 5, 39, 48, 49, 53, 54, 55, 56, 58, 61; Health and Welfare Services, 55
London Flower Mission, 56
London Metropolitan Archives, 5, 11
Lunardi, Vincent, 19
Luxborough Lodge (1949-65, formerly St Marylebone Institution 1930-49, St Marylebone Workhouse 1752-1930), 5, 53, 55, 56, 57, 58, **58**, **59**, 61; Inmates: Aged, 54; Infirm, 55; Diet, 54; Warden, 54, 56, 57; Maintenance and refurbishment, 54; Demolition, 55, 61
Luxborough Street, 7, 52, 54

MACLEAN Committee on Local Government, 49
Madame Tussaud, 5
Maitland, William, 6
Manning, Cardinal Henry Edward, 30, 39

Margate, 30
Marlesford Lodge (Kensington and Chelsea District School for younger children; now Palingswick House), 30
Martin, Edmund (Workhouse Master), 57
Marylebone High Street, 6
Marylebone Passage, 6
Marylebone Road, 8, 36, 39, 45, 48, 49, 52, 53, 61
McCulloch, Lieutenant John (inmate), 19
Metropolitan Asylums Board, 36, 37, 40, 48, 49
Metropolitan Board of Works, 31
Metropolitan Casual Paupers Order, 48
Metropolitan Common Poor Fund, 31, 37
Metropolitan Society for the Blind, 56
Middlesex, 17, 18
Miles, Sir Jonathan, 18
Mordaunt, Louisa (inmate), 25
Morrison, AC (Workhouse Master), 57
'Mouse buttocks', **13**
Mr Weekly's Metropolitan Establishment, 30
Muller, Franz, 34

NATIONAL ASSISTANCE BOARD, 48
National Health Service, 55
New Cavendish Street, 61
New Poor Law, 21, 22 (see also Acts of Parliament: Poor Law Amendment Act)
New Road, 8, 9, 11
Newgate Prison, 34
Nightingale, Florence, 40
North Hyde, Southall, 30
Northumberland Street (now Luxborough Street), 7, 9, 11, **12**, **35**, 36, **36**, 38, 39, 49, 54
Norwich Workhouse, 6

ORCHARDSON STREET (formerly Richmond Street), 37
Oxford, Earl of, 7
Oxford Street, 6, 8

PADDINGTON, 7, 8, 9, 11, 42, 49
Paddington Street, 7, 9, 11, 42
Paddington Workhouse, 49
Palingswick House (formerly Marlesford Lodge), 30
Parent, Francis (first Workhouse Master), 7
Parry, Johanna (inmate), 16
Pauperism, 8, 12, 30, 53
Paupers, 6, 7, 12, 14, 17, 18, 22, 34, 37, 43, 48, 53 (see also St Marylebone Workhouse: Inmates: Paupers)
Plymouth Workhouse, 6
Police Gazette, 23
Polytechnic of Central London (1970-92), 61 (see also Regent Street Polytechnic; Westminster, University of)
Poor Law, 5, 11, 22, 23, 25, 26, 27, 28, 29, 31, 37, 39, 43, 48; Poor Law Commissioners (1834-47), 22, 23, 25, 26; Poor Law Board (1847-71), 22, 26, 27, 28, 29, 31, 37, 39
Poor Man's Guardian Society, 25
Poor relief, 7, 9, 12, 16, 21, 22, 25, 42, 43, 48, 53; Outdoor, 6, 12, 14, 16, 22, 25, 42, 48
Poplar Workhouse, 43
Portland, Duke of, 9, **10**, 11
Portland Estate, 11, 38
Portman Estate, 11, 38
Portman, Henry, 9
Portman Mansions, 39

RACKHAM STREET (location of Ladbroke Grove Infirmary), 39
Red Cross, 54, 56

63

Regent Street Polytechnic (1882-1970), 55, 58; Buildings and layout, 61; Marylebone Road Site, 61; New Cavendish Street Site, 61; Regent Street Site, 61 (see also Polytechnic of Central London; Westminster, University of)
Rein, Thomas (Workhouse Master), 20, 57
Richmond Street (now Orchardson Street), 37
Rockett, William (Workhouse Master), 20, 57
Rocque's Map of London, 6
Rollinson, Ann (inmate), 16
Rowley, William, 11
Royal Commission on the Poor Laws and Relief of Distress, 48, 49
Royal Polytechnic Institution (1837-81), 58
Ryan, Richard (Workhouse Master), 26, 27, **27**, 57

SALISBURY, Mary (inmate), 7
Sanders, Sarah (inmate), 16
Senior, William (Workhouse Master), 57
Sheppard, Dr FHW, 5
Sheppard, Jack, 19
Simmonds, Nevil Mark (Workhouse Master), 57
Simmonds, Reginald George (Workhouse Master), 57
Sims, George R, **46**, **47**
Smallpox Hospital (Highgate), 36
Smith, Dr E, 39
Snell, Alfred Saxon, 43
Snell, H Saxon, 36, 38, 40, 42, 43
Somerset House, 22, 23
Southall (location of St Marylebone Workhouse schools), 30, 37
Southwark, 53
Spanish Place Chapel, 39
St Charles Hospital (formerly Ladbroke Grove Infirmary), 40

64

St George's parish, 8
St Giles-in-the-Fields, 6
St Marylebone Borough Council, 52
St Marylebone Burial ground, 7, 8, 9, 11, 42
St Marylebone Institution (1930-49, formerly St Marylebone Workhouse 1752-1930; later Luxborough Lodge 1949-65), 49, 52, 53
St Marylebone Old People's Committee, 56
St Marylebone poorhouse (1730-52, later St Marylebone Workhouse), 6
St Marylebone Society, 5
St Marylebone Volunteers, 19
St Marylebone Workhouse (1752-1930, later St Marylebone Institution 1930-49, then Luxborough Lodge 1949-65), 5, 6, **10**, 12, **12**, 17, 18, 19, 22, 23, 27, 29, 31, **31**, **32**, **33**, **35**, 36, **36**, 37, 39, **40**, **41**, 43, **44**, 45, 48, 49, 57; Old (1752-1775), 11; New (1775-1930), 9, 11;
  Account of work, **13**;
  Advertisements, **7**, **13**;
  Administrative bodies: Open Vestry (to 1768), 6, 7, 8; Rota Committee, 11, 16; Select Vestry (1768-1832), 8, 9, 11, 21; Vestry (after 1832), 21, 29, 37, 42; Directors and Guardians of the Poor (1775-1867), 5, 9, 11, 12, 14, 16, 17, 18, 19, 20, 21, 22, 23, 25, 26, 27, 28, 29, 30, 36, 37, 38, 42, 57; Board of Guardians (1867-1930), 5, 37, 38; Workhouse Reconstruction Committee, 38, 39, 40;
  Buildings and wards: Able-bodied men's accommodation, 20, 45, 54; Able-bodied women's accommodation, 42, 53; Alexandra Ward for mentally ill men, 45; Casual Wards, **34**, **35**, 38, 39, 45, 48;

Central Administrative Block, 39; Chapel, **10**, 11, 20, **32**, **33**, 38, 39, 45; 'The Cottage', 28; Dining Hall, **46**; Dorcas Ward for mentally ill women, 45; Infirm Wards, **36**; Laundry Block, 52; Lying-in Wards, 40; Male and Female Nightly Asylums for vagrants, 23; Maternity Ward, 45, 52; Mental Observation Wards, 45, 52; New Central Relief Station, **50**, **51**; Old relief station, 54; Nursery, 20, 30, 52; Prison Cells, 19; Refractory Women's Ward, 26; Vagrant Wards, 31;
Buildings, layout and maintenance, 7, 11, 18, 20, **34**, 36, 37, 38, 40, 42, 43, 45, 48, 55;
Conditions, 8, 25, 31, 34;
Diet, 8, 16, 17, 26, 34, 54; Officers', 17; Provisioning costs 17; Tables, Appendix A
Discipline, 8, 16, 18, 26, 27, 42;
Education, 7, 8, 14, 20, 26, 29, 30, 37; Schools, 14, 29; Boys' school, 20, 29, 30; Girls' school, 20, 26, 29, 30; Infants' school, 29, 30; Curriculum and timetable, 29, 30; (for schools on other locations, see Southall, Banstead, Marlesford Lodge, Walthamstow)
Finances, 17, 20, 21, 22, 25, 26, 31; 49;
Health, 9, 11, 12, 20, 36, 37, 40, 45; (see also St Marylebone Workhouse: Infirmary, Ladbroke Grove Infirmary, Inmates: Aged and infirm);
Infirmary, 11, 12, 14, **15**, 17, 18, 20, 25, 26, 38, 39, 40; Apothecary, 14; Matron or Head Nurse, 14; Nurses, 14; Patients, 20; Physician, 11, 14; Surgeon, 14, 16 (see also St Marylebone Workhouse: Ladbroke Grove Infirmary);